Ants in Their Pants

ANTS IN THEIR PANTS

Teaching Children Who Must Move to Learn

AERIAL CROSS

Redleaf Press®
www.redleafpress.org
800-423-8309

Published by Redleaf Press
10 Yorkton Court
St. Paul, MN 55117
www.redleafpress.org

The author and Redleaf Press have made every effort to trace and contact the copyright holders of all materials reprinted in this book. If there are any inadvertent omissions, we apologize to those concerned and ask that they contact Redleaf Press at info@redleafpress.org so that we can correct any oversight as soon as possible.

First edition 2010
Cover design by Elizabeth Berry
Interior typeset in Berkeley and designed by Erin Kirk New
Interior photos courtesy of the author
ASL artwork on pages 73 through 79 courtesy of Becky Radtke
Illustrations on the last appendix page courtesy of Elizabeth Bub
Developmental edit by Kristen Kunkel
Printed in the United States of America
17 16 15 14 13 12 11 10 2 3 4 5 6 7 8 9

Library of Congress Cataloging-in-Publication Data
Cross, Aerial.
    Ants in their pants : teaching children who must move to learn / Aerial Cross.
        p. cm.
    Includes bibliographical references.
    ISBN 978-1-933653-87-7
    1. Hyperactive children—Education (Early childhood) 2. Movement education—Study and teaching (Early childhood)—Activity programs. 3. Sensorimotor integration. I. Title.
    LC4711.C76 2009
    371.94—dc22
                                        2008053531

FSC
Mixed Sources
Product group from well-managed forests and other controlled sources
Cert no. SW-COC-002283
www.fsc.org
© 1996 Forest Stewardship Council

Printed on FSC certified paper

This book is dedicated to my four older brothers:
Charley, John, Chris, and Jim.

Your busy little sister loves you!

Ants in Their Pants

2   An Extra Busy Child's Best Environment   55

3   Working with Extra Busy Children   69

4   Ready, Set, Play   101

Acknowledgments

Phil—You never stopped believing in me, busyness and all.
Thank you for your love, support, and patience.

PJ, Farrah, and li'l extra busy Bella—You are truly gifts from above.
I am blessed to be your mother.

Sarah—I miss you.

Stephanie, Julie, Eileen, Michelle, and Shawn—The power of
girlfriends and networking mamas!

Andrew Fine and Jack L. Fortner—Thank you for being you.

Kristen, Kyra, and David—Thank you for doing what you do
best . . . editing!

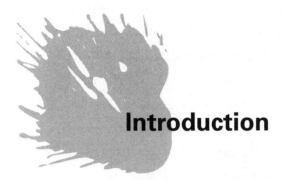

Introduction

I once heard, "To write well, you should write about what you know well." I know extra busy kinesthetically natured children. I was one . . . and it's been a busy thirty-six years! As a child, and to this day, I am most tranquil when in motion. Like kinesthetic children, I am happiest doing whatever I am doing—moving.

From a parental perspective, my husband and I are blessed with three beautiful, healthy, and precocious children—ages fifteen, twelve, and six. We understand how raising an overly active child can be trying. Our third child, Isabella, or Bella, is dynamically driven and has been since birth. Extra busy remains her story. She sticks to it daily. As an educator, I have been privileged to teach extra busy children of all ages and exceptionalities for over a decade. During this time, I have witnessed many parents and colleagues become overwhelmed with the demanding nature of kinesthetic children.

Why I Wrote This Book

I ventured into writing *Ants in Their Pants: Teaching Children Who Must Move to Learn* largely because my most memorable teaching moments as an educator and special educator have been those in which I have assisted extra busy kinesthetic children to channel or redirect their excess energy in a positive direction. I wanted to share my ideas and help and inform others working with these little whirlwinds.

Ants in Their Pants is meant to inspire and foster support for those working with children who must move to learn. It is full of simple and sensory-integrated ideas for accommodating or designing a productive schedule for an extra busy kinesthetically natured student or child. The Strengthening the Home-School Connection tidbits offered throughout the book relay the importance of continuous teamwork and open communication between parents and educators when working with extra busy children. Unlike other idea books, *Ants in Their Pants* is personal, easy to read, and straightforward. It is meant to help educators and child care providers channel a kinesthetic child's excess energy in a positive direction without extinguishing the child's flame of individuality while remaining sane.

Ants in Their Pants is based on my

- experiences as a mother of an active kinesthetic child named Bella;
- experience as a special educator teaching children with severe and mild exceptionalities, including autism, Asperger's syndrome, attention deficit disorder (ADD), attention deficit/ hyperactivity disorder (ADHD), traumatic brain injury, Down syndrome, or another specific learning disability;
- experience as an educator working with kindergarteners, preschoolers, second graders, and young English-language learners;
- upbringing and experiences as child number seven in a family of thirteen very different children; and
- being a child advocate who wants to see all children happy, healthy, and marching to the beat of their own little drum.

How to Get the Most Out of This Book

I wrote *Ants in Their Pants* in a purposefully quick, been-there-done-that (BTDT) format, referring often to my experiences with extra busy kinesthetic children in my classroom and on the home front.

Five more to come—
I'm second from the right.

To get the most out of this book, I suggest first skimming the section What "Ants in Their Pants" Means on page 6, where I explain my interpretation of the nature of an extra busy kinesthetic child. Grappling with this interpretation will help you comprehend the book better, ultimately enabling you to more readily help extra busy kinesthetic children.

Throughout the book I offer ideas to help you fill a Busy Bag— a toolbox of strategies, insights, and resources. One of my hopes is that you will see the importance of rotating through, sharing, and referring to this book as much as possible on those white-knuckle, rubber-hits-the-road days. Strengthening the Home-School Connection tidbits are meant to fill your Busy Bag too—one can never have too many ideas when working with kinesthetic children. Also, I'd like to add that when I refer to "parents" throughout the book, I am referring to individuals who parent a child, including grandparents, aunts, uncles, or other extended family members. Parenting is one of life's biggest challenges; it is a job that requires a community of support, especially if the child is curious, extra precocious, and has a hands-on kinesthetic nature. Regardless of its makeup, the term "parents" denotes those individuals involved in the act of parenting.

To Survive, Get Out of the Box

I'm an out-of-the-box thinker, willing to try almost anything to make a child healthy, happy at home, and successful in the classroom. I recommend continual out-of-the-box thinking and remind educators and parents that just because something worked on Monday doesn't guarantee it will work on Tuesday, or any other day of the week for that matter. The following two stories should explain my particular viewpoint.

Story 1: When Bella was two-and-a-half years old, for some reason she found comfort and enjoyment sitting in her empty infant bathing tub. I'll never forget how her cute, chubby build fit snugly within it. After lunch one afternoon, she wanted a few leftover spaghetti noodles to nibble on while she sat in the tub stacking blocks. I indulged her. She stacked and slurped away for about five minutes before her extra busy nature reasserted itself.

In the short time it took me to walk from the kitchen to my bedroom, drop my rings on my vanity, and walk back again, Bella had taken the bowl of noodles from the countertop and dumped them into her tiny tub. I reentered the kitchen to discover her squishing and jiggling warm, wet noodles between her fingers and toes, squealing with delight. I was speechless. At first I scolded her and quickly cleaned up the mess. The following day, however, I noticed her eyeing a bowl of jumbo shells.

"What the heck?" I thought.

And from then on, to her delight, three to four times a week I cleaned out the tub, put down a drop cloth, and dumped a batch of lukewarm, sticky noodles into it. This activity proved itself worthwhile and educational. I thought Bella was one of the luckiest toddlers on the block, attempting to pronounce "whole wheat," "linguini," and "fettuccini" and exploring their different textures. I especially enjoyed watching her put oversized rigatoni noodles on each finger and exclaim, "Mommy, look!" and then slurp them off her pudgy digits one by one. Many of my friends found the activity

Busy Bag Trick
Quit worrying about what others deem pertinent, much less what the latest trend seems to be. Concentrate on being as creative, hands-on, and sensory-integrated as possible. Lock into the child's personality, interests, and learning style.

wasteful and messy, and saw it as teaching my child to play with her food. We agreed to disagree.

Story 2: Bella was colicky from birth to three months of age. She cried continually from about 6:00 to 9:00 nightly. It was a difficult time, to say the least. Fortunately, a girlfriend of mine saved us with an unusual tip: "Aerial," she said, "do exactly as I suggest. It got me through Haley's crying spells. Wrap Bella snugly in a light blanket, put her in her infant carrying seat, and set it on top of your dryer. Put one of your husband's shoes inside and turn it on air dry." Amazingly, the vibrating dryer and loud thudding of the shoe calmed Bella. I quickly wrote down the idea and have since passed it on many times.

It's important to remember that as you start thinking outside the box, surviving a kinesthetic child's nature will come more easily. It will become second nature. Networking with friends, educators, colleagues, and parents to gain new ideas is also extremely helpful. Ultimately though, focus on what's best for the child. Anecdotally log the outcomes of your trials—triumphs and flops. Chances are you'll look back one day, read them, and laugh.

Busy Bag Trick
Teaching extra busy kinesthetic children isn't easy. Realize you can only do your best. Consider setbacks little lessons that can go toward stuffing your Busy Bag.

What "Ants in Their Pants" Means

When I refer to children as having ants in their pants or being extra busy, I mean young children who are natural kinesthetic learners, who *must* move to learn. Extra busy kinesthetic children are rearing to go, go, go, and they continuously want to know why, why, why. Extra busy kinesthetic children are often precocious and have larger-than-life personalities. They see life as a daily series of miraculous experiences and are often known as being bright eyed and bushy tailed. At times their curiosity seems unstoppable.

Let's look more closely at characteristics of very active children. Extra busy children move excessively due to a kinesthetic nature. This nature is driven by intense curiosity, a need for continual tactile experiences, and the requirement to move in order to concentrate and learn. It demands environments, schedules, and guidelines for using excess energy that are different from traditional teaching or parenting methods.

Extra busy kinesthetic learners are naturally more active and have more physical energy to expend than other children. They often display habits common to extra busy children. These habits can be trying at times, but not for long periods of time. Extra busy habits can be managed with consistency, creativity, sensory-integrated tools and techniques, varied play, and a structured environment that incorporates proper sleep and nutrition.

Busy Personalities

I highly recommend a wonderful children's personality book for your Busy Bag: *The Treasure Tree* by John Trent, Judith DuFour Love, and Cindy Trent (1998). This beautifully illustrated book uses four animals—an otter, a lion, a beaver, and a golden retriever—to describe four basic personalities of children. According to *The Treasure Tree* my children can be described as follows.

Phillip James, "PJ," is fifteen. He fits the description of an otter. Otters love to socialize, a key characteristic of this personality type.

PJ is popular at school, loved by everyone, and can easily work a crowd. Like otters, PJ tends to rush through things (especially his homework), paying little attention to detail. He loves to hang out in his messy room (otters are notorious for untidy rooms), listening to music or talking on the phone.

Next in line is twelve-year-old Farrah. She has a golden retriever personality. Retrievers are loving, sensitive, and empathetic. They make friends easily but do not readily welcome change. Reassurance is important to golden retrievers. Farrah, like a retriever, is a people pleaser—very helpful, loyal, quiet, and melodious.

Now Isabella. Bella is our roaring six-year-old lion cub. She is goal oriented, forceful, and insistent. When Bella sets her mind on something, watch out! Lions tend to boss everyone around. They often display a my-way-or-the-highway attitude. Bella keeps us on our toes with "Let's do it now!" Lion personalities are also fearless and vibrantly vocal.

As you ponder each child's personality, keep in mind Dr. Lawrence Shapiro's statement that a young personality is about 49 percent nature and 51 percent nurture (2003, 3). The four types described in the book are only a spectrum for categorizing personalities. Granting that a "lotter" (a lion-otter combination) or "golden beaver" (golden retriever–beaver combination) may exist a few days out of the week, the book targets the child's strongest characteristics. *The Treasure Tree* also has a helpful checklist to fill out to learn more about a child's individual personality strengths.

What All Children Need, Especially Extra Busy Kinesthetic Children

An extra busy child often reminds me of a puppy, needing guidance, constant supervision, and plenty of creative and supportive chew toys to get through the day.

Luck plays no part in positively raising or teaching these children. They require an extra helping of everything, especially

unconditional love
quality and quantity time
consistency
security

Each of these needs intertwines with three additional needs.

Unconditional Love	Quality and Quantity Time	Consistency	Security
Acceptance	Consistent	Routines	Support
Affirmation	Continuous	Reasons	Strength
Affection	Care	Rules	Speech

Strengthening the Home-School Connection

In a newsletter for families, consider making these suggestions: Rise early enough to get ready before the children wake. This will allow for an attentive breakfast with chit-chat about the upcoming day or a few morning cuddles. Go out on a family date together. Remember, children are only small for a brief period. Enjoy this time—you'll never get it back.

Unconditional Love

Extra busy children need daily doses of unconditional love expressed through the three A's—acceptance, affirmation, and affection. Giving daily doses of the three A's not only expresses and models unconditional love but also helps extra busy children grow into loving, confident individuals. Make it obvious to an extra busy child that she is an accepted, honored member of the group. Give praise when appropriate, being careful not to build false pride—too much praise can backfire. Ways to express unconditional love appear throughout the book. Here are some to get you started:

- Set limits, boundaries, and rules for an extra busy child to exist within. Consistently stick to them!
- Enforce consequences for behaving inappropriately and disregarding established rules.
- Listen and talk to the child attentively throughout the day.
- Maintain constant, deep eye contact when speaking with the child.
- Never compare children to one another.

Quality and Quantity Time

There is no better investment than spending time with a child. Children need daily doses of quality and quantity time expressed through the three C's: consistency, continuity, and care. Try not to confuse quality time and quantity time; they are not the same. Twenty minutes of focused attention speaks volumes more than an hour of just being in the same room watching television together, for example. Here are some more ideas that will allow you to spend quality and quantity time with children:

- Be a multitasker.
- Hold regular classroom meetings.
- Cut back and learn to say no.
- Arrive fifteen to twenty minutes before the children to prepare for the school day, and make copies beforehand.
- Leave your classroom ready for the next school day.

Consistency

Extra busy children and consistency go together like peanut butter and jelly. Yes, it's that important! Extra busy children not only need consistency, they thrive on it. A predictable, structured home and classroom make an extra busy child feel safe, secure, and loved.

Extra busy children need daily doses of consistency expressed through the three R's: routines, reasons, and rules. Consistent routines give extra busy children a sense of stability. Rules establish boundaries, limits, and respect for others as well as health and safety guidelines. Rules should be reasonable and explainable. Children can benefit from understanding age-appropriate, realistic reasoning behind rules and limits. For example, "Paul, we use glue sticks during math time because glue sticks are not as messy as bottled glue. We use bottled glue for our art projects." One reason is enough; thereafter give a response similar to this: "Because I am your teacher, and I have set this guideline." Here are two more ideas for beefing up consistency:

- Post a schedule and follow it.
- Question what your "no" really means. Is it wishy-washy or firm? Do your students walk right over it, or do they know you mean business when you say it?

Busy Bag Trick

Post an extra busy child's daily schedule. Try to establish a sense of structure and purpose for each day. Make sure the schedule is understandable to him. For prereaders, including pictures with the schedule is helpful. Posted schedules work well at school and at home.

Busy Bag Trick

A child who hears "no" a hundred times a day will eventually tune it out. Use it sparingly.

Security

Secure children prosper developmentally. An extra busy child will naturally feel secure if her needs for love, time, and consistency are met. Granting an extra busy child security is possible with daily doses of the three S's: support, strength, and speech.

Extra busy children need a sense of group identity. A sense of belonging will strengthen their confidence and give them security during times of change or intense transitioning. Extra busy children feel support when a network of friends or extended family is present. A gentle, enthusiastic, yet firm teacher can provide ample security for an extra busy kinesthetic child as well. To help strengthen children's security

- Prepare extra busy children for change. If you are aware of an upcoming intense transition like a field trip or a substitute teacher, let the child know in advance. Springing things on extra busy children can be difficult.
- Take care of yourself. You will be more productive as a parent or educator if you take care of yourself. This includes eating right, exercising regularly, getting adequate sleep, relying on a support network, and taking time for you.

Busy Bag Trick
Extra busy children are successful in the classroom and at home if busy behaviors are addressed and viewed from all angles by everyone. All parties need to work together. Encourage family members to offer tips about what is working at home, where control over the child's environment is easier. Every attempt should be made by educators to be receptive and flexible with suggestions.

Ten Common Characteristics of Extra Busy Kinesthetic Children

I've experienced ten characteristics common to extra busy kinesthetic children, ages one through eight, and outlined them here. The characteristics are often outgrown, or they become milder as the child ages. The characteristics seldom cause failure in school if tackled quickly, properly, consistently, and creatively. The characteristics intertwine but tend to work in intense sets of three—with excessive movement often taking the number one spot.

Excessive movement remains Bella's number one extra busy characteristic. Bella's number two characteristic is her noisiness.

Whether transitioning, eating, playing, or brushing her teeth, Bella is making noise—humming, giggling, singing, gurgling, blowing raspberries, popping her cheek. Stubbornness is her number three characteristic. Bella's strong-willed. She demands choices and explanations for her boundaries, even after the hundredth time I have explained them. Bella struggles with many of the other extra busy characteristics off and on. Staying on top of her excessive movement, noise, and stubbornness is most important though. If this doesn't happen, those three become problematic, revving up the rest.

These are ten characteristics common among extra busy children. Each is described in detail on the following pages.

1. excessive movement
2. variable attention span
3. distractible
4. careless
5. disorganized
6. difficulty transitioning
7. coarse manners
8. noisy
9. spontaneous
10. strong-willed

Extra Busy Children Often Move Excessively

Children who are kinesthetically natured need to move, and they use many methods to do this in the classroom. I have heard the following during my years as a regular kindergarten and second grade teacher and primary special educator:

- "I need another drink of water."
- "I left something in my backpack. Can I get it?"
- "I think it's starting to rain, Mrs. Cross. Can I check?"
- "My pencil is dull. It needs to be sharpened again."
- "I have to use the restroom again, Mrs. Cross."
- "Mrs. Cross, I dropped my pencil across the room again."
- "Look, Mrs. Cross, the leaves are changing colors. Can I look at them?"

Other forms of extra busy movement I've observed at home or school include

- head shaking or foot shaking while working;
- walking around the classroom unnecessarily;
- running in the house or halls;
- squirming, shifting, fidgeting, or wriggling while seated; and
- pacing or dancing while waiting in line.

Extra busy kinesthetic children can also display excessive physical movement through simple motor tics or unintentional rapid, repetitious behaviors, such as

- head jerking;
- bobbing back and forth;
- eye blinking, rolling, or twitching;
- tongue chewing and wagging, or letting it hang out; and
- odd facial expressions, neck thrusts, or nose scrunching.

Here are some ideas for redirecting or minimizing excessive movement:

- Allow regular breaks for movement. I list several in chapter 2.
- Allow the child to carry a fidget toy. A fidget toy is a small item of interest (to the child) used to occupy his hands and thoughts during downtime in or out of the classroom. A small koosh ball is a perfect example of a fidget toy. I list several other ideas in chapter 3. Visit www.southpawenterprises.com for additional fidget toy products and suggestions.
- Borrow a stretchy band (similar to a large rubber band) from a school occupational therapist. Stretch it across the child's desk for him to fiddle with while seated. This technique can also be used at the dinner table or even at a restaurant. Stretchy bands aren't noisy or distracting, yet they allow fidgeting movement for comfort.
- Ask to have a rocking chair placed in the classroom. Give the child a five-minute rocking break with a book or fidget toy. Rocking chairs are valuable at home, too.
- Do not take away recess time as a means of discipline. This will only make excessive movement matters worse. Making

the swings or monkey bars off limits is a better option. The restriction should be enforced with consistency.

Extra Busy Children Often Have Variable Attention Spans

For most extra busy children, paying attention is difficult, especially when it comes to things like doing homework, cleaning up, sitting down to eat, or following along in a book. They quickly lose interest or their minds wander. One of the easiest ways to accommodate inattentive children is to keep activities fast paced, upbeat, bold, fresh, and creative. Here are some more ideas for accommodating variable attention spans:

- Attempt to create a quiet environment while the child is working by turning off the radio, TV, video games, and computer.
- Highlight or circle information on the chalkboard or in homework. Arrows, underlining, or colored quotations marks are helpful too.
- Encourage parents to sit with their child or cook dinner while he does his homework nearby.
- Primary-school teachers can stay nearby or walk up and down the aisles while the child completes seated work. Ask follow-up or refocusing questions, such as "How's it coming?"
- Try positive reinforcement: "Wow! You are almost done!" Refrain from "Hurry up! What's taking you so long? I just showed you!"
- Help the extra busy child build on his attention span. Slowly add time to tasks or length to assignments. Here are some suggestions for activities that can increase attention span in the classroom or at home:
  —Play memory games or work with puzzles, increasing the number of pieces each time you play.
  —Cook a meal or make a simple snack from a step-by-step recipe.
  —Put together model airplanes. Start easy and then increase the level of difficulty.

—Try yoga. (Yoga has even been suggested by occupational therapists I have worked with.)

—Take regular stretch breaks in the classroom.

—Explain directions slowly and simply. Be specific. For example, "Put your book in your desk after you are done eating" is more helpful than "Put your book away."

—Hide a ticking clock and let the child find it (Whelchel 2000).

Extra Busy Children Often Are Easily Distracted

All children are distracted at some point during the day. The extra busy child, however, unintentionally notices simple details and noises that other children naturally block out. Some are obvious, such as other children, the radio, or the TV. Some are not so obvious, such as the pencil movement of the child in the seat behind her, the smell of the teacher's hairspray, or an open window allowing odd sounds inside. Here are some ideas for helping extra busy children focus:

- Ask parents to complete a detailed profile card that lists possible distractions.
- Encourage parents to keep the child's backpack clutter free. Remove unnecessary items daily.
- Suggest to parents that the child's clothing be simple. Shirts with big bright buttons or suspenders can be tempting to fiddle with during class. As an educator and parent, I've discovered that simple pullover shirts and sturdy Velcro tennis shoes work best. Boots and flip flops seldom go over well with extra busy children.
- Purchase a copy of *Where's Waldo?* by Martin Handford (1997). Sit with the child and try to find Waldo together. This book series is excellent for honing focusing skills. Scholastic's *I Spy* books work well too.
- Play searching games with the child. For example, hide a small object from the child and have her find it by giving one clue, such as "It's under something blue." Gradually add clues. "It's under something blue near the bookshelf. . . .

Strengthening the Home-School Connection

Invite parents to visit classrooms prior to the beginning of the school year to identify the teacher who would be the best match for their child. As stated earlier, the teacher needs to be willing to work consistently, yet gently, with the child's focusing challenges.

It's under something blue on the table near the bookshelf." Enhance the game for readers by writing the clues on different pieces of paper so that each one directs the child to the next.

- Play Telephone, a game that encourages listening skills. (You will need at least four people.) Sit in a circle. Select somebody to start the call by whispering a phrase in the next person's ear. Continue until the call returns to the person who started it. See if the call made it through without errors in the phrase.
- Play aiming games, such as suction-cup darts or securely pin up a small wicker or wooden basket and play basketball games with a soft foam ball.
- Lay out three or four objects that would resonate differently, such as a tall glass, an aluminum can, a plastic tub, and a shoe box. Have the child close her eyes and guess which object you strike.

Extra Busy Children Often Are Careless

An extra busy child can be careless, accident prone, and at times appear as though he seldom thinks before he acts. Most of this carelessness is due to daydreaming and thinking in ten different directions at once. Here are some ways to minimize carelessness:

- Make sure the child understands what you are asking him to do and the sequence of steps for accomplishing a desired task. Although it sounds overly simplified, lay out the steps precisely. For example, "This is how we line up for recess. First, I call a table of children. Second, that table quietly stands up and pushes in their chairs. Third, that table of students walks quietly to the door. Then I call a second table of children." You may do this with words, pictures, hand-over-hand guidance, or modeling depending mostly on the child's strengths and weaknesses as well as on how he is presently performing the task (Mauro and Cermak 2006).

Busy Bag Trick
I recommend Terri Mauro and Sharon Cermak's book *The Everything Parent's Guide to Sensory Integration Disorder.* Mauro and Cermak thoroughly discuss the issues distractible children have and suggests ways to "destress" clothing among other things.

- Be realistic about the child's abilities. Is the material or concept too difficult? If the child isn't ready for a tall glass, continue with a cup. If the child can't add, she will falter at multiplication.
- Play up the child's strengths to overcome carelessness. Let the child regularly experience success.

Extra Busy Children Often Are Disorganized

In the overall picture of excessive busyness, organizational skills were the least of my worries as an educator. Nevertheless, I do understand how lack of organization can prove problematic as a child grows. The following are ideas for helping children become more organized:

- For younger children, color code buckets or bins for toys at home and school.
- For school-age children, clearly mark a place in a folder or binder for the child to store homework. Ask parents to check with their child to make sure completed homework is in its place when she leaves for school in the morning. Check homework folders just before the child leaves school.
- Guide organization as much as possible. As the child gets older and less distracted by busyness, you can teach her the techniques that work best for her individually.
- Parents can place a hamper for dirty clothes in the child's room and enforce its use.
- Help the child keep her backpack and desk clutter free. Provide time in the morning or at the end of the day for the child to organize them, pockets and drawers included.
- Minimize materials in her desk.
- Designate a spot in the classroom for recess gear, such as balls, jump ropes, or Frisbees. Encourage parents to do the same for recreation gear at home.

Extra Busy Children Often Have Difficulty Transitioning

Our extra busy Bella doesn't have a problem starting a new task.
It's stopping the old one that ruffles her feathers. In addition to
the two ideas below, there are transitioning ideas in chapter 3.

- Sing while transitioning. Singing is a developmentally appropriate practice for extra busy children. Songs welcoming busy
bees to circle time or to cleanup time naturally create a softer
mood, and they help keep kinesthetic children focused as they
move from one activity to the next. Many children's songs,
jingles, and fingerplays are intentionally repetitious, perfect for
extra busy children needing patterned steps to stop and shift.
Use traditional songs and movements to embrace transitioning
routines; sing high, low, softly, and loudly. I suggest many song
possibilities in chapter 5.

- Use a buddy system for transitioning. Children often help one
another, and they can create solutions for their own problems
at times. Creatively use a buddy system to help children move
from one activity to another. Pair or group students according
to strengths, weaknesses, or complementary abilities. Have
buddies take turns giving directions for starting activities, as
well as ending and shifting them.

Extra Busy Children Often Are Coarsely Mannered

Some of the most common coarse behaviors I've seen in extra busy
kinesthetic children are

- poor table manners,
- inappropriate language,
- grabbing at things without permission,
- interrupting others,
- talking while others are talking,
- pulling on parents while they are talking,
- invading someone's space without an "Excuse me," and
- bothering others who are trying to work.

Teaching children—disabled, busy, gifted—manners and respect for others is important. Whatever the characteristics of the precious package, I find they're not a part of parenting or educating that we get to pick and choose. Here are some ideas for redirecting poor manners:

- Play out scenarios. Walk through the steps of the manners desired—together! (This is also very helpful for dealing with carelessness.) Be as specific as possible, clearly illustrating what is acceptable and not acceptable. Practice over and over if needed.
  - —"This is how you eat at the table."
  - —"This is how you will gain my attention during class time."
  - —"This is how you will not attempt to gain my attention."
- Coach by modeling manners. The following are some general manners extra busy children may need coaching on.
  - —Extra busy children often disregard physical space boundaries for standing and speaking with others. They often intrude carelessly on the personal space of others.
  - —Extra busy children may need to be taught how to use a fork, spoon, and knife properly. They may also need to be shown how to carry on a conversation properly while enjoying a meal with others.
  - —Extra busy children may need to be shown how to wait for a turn patiently.
  - —Extra busy children may need to be shown how to open doors for others.
- Excessive movement can appear ill-mannered at times. Refer to chapter 3 for fidget-toy ideas.
- Let the child release excess energy through strenuous physical exercise before scheduled outings. Refer to chapter 4 for physical play ideas.
- Use story books to discuss the use and power of proper manners. Here are some books I recommend for working on manners:

—Caring behavior: *The Ant and the Elephant* by Bill Peet (1972)

—Courtesy: *Clifford's Manners* by Norman Bridwell (1987)

—Fairness: *Me First* by Helen Lester (1995)

—Perseverance when frustrated: *The Little Engine That Could* by Watty Piper (2005)

—Responsibility for actions: *Horton Hatches the Egg* by Dr. Seuss (1968)

- Extra busy children often have trouble cooperating with other children on the playground. They can be bossy. Let the child experience playtime when the playground isn't so crowded. Stay out an extra five to ten minutes after other classes have gone inside. Use the extra time to guide and redirect appropriate social manners and behavior.

Extra Busy Children Often Are Noisy

Besides constant movement, extra busy children are known for making boisterous and unruly sounds, usually at the most inopportune times imaginable. Believe it or not, an extra busy child's activities come alive when accompanied with loud, animated sounds. And most of the time, the child is completely unaware of the intensity; it's just natural for a truck to go *vroom*— loudly! Although many of Bella's noises can test my patience, I focus on the volume of the noise more than the noise itself. She often turns her babbling sounds into singing, or skipping. Extra busy kinesthetic children often display noisy vocal tics, repetitious behaviors they engage in unintentionally. As a teacher, parent, and aunt (as a sister to twelve, I have lots of nieces and nephews), I have seen the following vocal tics in extra busy children:

- clearing the throat or coughing when not needed
- snorting, sniffling
- humming
- burping

Busy Bag Trick

A fabulous way to gather possible playmates on the playground is to let a child roll a ball up an unoccupied slide and let it roll back down. For some reason, whenever Bella initiates this game at the park, other children swarm to her asking, "Can I try?"

The following are some ideas for redirecting unnecessary noises or tics:

- Interest the child in creating crazy animal sounds. "Oh sure," you're thinking, "a barking extra busy child is all I need." The idea is to transform the unwanted noise into a game of animal sounds. "What sound does a cow make? What sound does a rooster make? What animal says bow-wow? Baa baa? Buzz buzz? Cock-a-doodle-doo?"
- Teach and sing nursery rhymes with the child. Interrupt an annoying loud noise with "Let's sing 'Little Miss Muffet'" or just start singing "Pop Goes the Weasel." Children love the "pop."
- Rhyming games work wonders. Children can easily be drawn into these. Invent funny names or phrases for objects or family members. "Bella knew a fella who had a sister named Stella." "Dad is rad!" Dr. Seuss books are a resource for these.
- Turn to chapter 3 for additional ideas.

Extra Busy Children Often Are Spontaneous

Extra busy children often have spontaneous habits with regard to impatience or difficulty taking turns. They often react immediately to situations or have trouble waiting for assistance in the classroom. Here are some ideas for handling excessive spontaneity:

- Make the extra busy child aware of what he is doing incorrectly, and what is needed to do it correctly. "We are not drawing now. We are working on our math seatwork now. You may draw after your seatwork is done. I can't wait to let you draw once your math work is done." Be calm, clear, and consistent.
- Provide constant positive reinforcement for positive behavior. Ignore attention-seeking behavior. This is difficult at times, but possible.
- Don't place emphasis on perfection. Keep the climate of the classroom and home noncompetitive.
- Let the child have a fidget toy when needed. See chapter 3 for ideas.

- Always make direct eye contact with the child when speaking. Use the child's name. "Katrina, I will be with you right after I finish helping Roy." It is also helpful to kneel or squat down to the child's level for a more personal face-to-face conversation.
- Give the child a task or activity while he is waiting. I've found clay to be a successful waiting material in and out of the classroom.
- Have the child explain back the directions. "Jack, we are leaving for music time in ten minutes, and you need to finish your work. What do you need to do in ten minutes, Jack?"
- Ask if the child has questions. Do so more than once.
- Have a sibling or peer help the child.
- Make sure the child is well aware of house and classroom rules, expectations, and consequences.

Extra Busy Children Often Are Strong-Willed

Having a strong-willed child can be exhausting, especially if the child happens to be extra busy. I intentionally listed strong-willed as characteristic number ten because, although extra busy children require consistency, a strong-willed extra busy child requires an even firmer consistent hand. If this habit is left unattended, the other nine habits will more than likely ensue, in chaos.

Taming, not breaking, a kinesthetic nature is possible with consistency, and make sure the child knows who's in charge—you! Children obey the adults in their lives, not the other way around. Establishing control as a parent or educator is vital. Resources I recommend for supporting a strong-willed child include the following:
- All About Parenting (www.allaboutparenting.org), practical information for surviving with strong-willed children
- *You Can't Make Me (But I Can Be Persuaded): Strategies for Bringing Out the Best in Your Strong-Willed Child* by Cynthia Ulrich Tobias (1999)
- *Aaron's Way: The Journey of a Strong-Willed Child* by Kendra Smiley (2004)

- *The New Strong-Willed Child: Birth through Adolescence* by James Dobson (2004)

The Most Powerful Teaching Tool for Extra Busy Children

In spring 2006, I ventured toward a doctorate in education at the University of New Mexico. One of the first educational theories I absorbed was this: modeling is the most powerful teaching tool. Modeling—consciously acting in a specific way in the hope you will be imitated—is a scientifically well-documented method of teaching new behaviors. "The process of modeling is most effective when the model itself is successful" (Franzini 2002, 60).

Luckily, it doesn't take a PhD to comprehend that small children mimic words and eventually grow to imitate attitudes and values of those within their environment. After looking at an extra busy child's nature, needs, personality, and learning preference, I recommend looking at what you are modeling. What are your day in, day out habits?

Your daily words and actions mold the way a child perceives herself, others, and the world. The daily events surrounding your life affect the lives of children, shaping their behavior and future.

A Word of Caution

Children see right through character charades. They more readily learn, adapt to, and repeat what they continually see versus what they continually hear. Here are a few examples of charades:
- Do you nag an extra busy child about sugar consumption yet continually eat junk food in front of him?
- Are you stressing the importance of exercising and getting outside, yet being a coach potato?
- Do you insist that the extra busy child keep his volume down in the classroom, yet often raise yours to get his attention?
- Do you maintain that the child shouldn't take what isn't his, yet

you take everything not nailed down in your hotel room when traveling?

I do not present the above to spark guilt—only awareness. Actions speak volumes more than words.

Finally, as you venture through *Ants in Their Pants,* relax. You can truly make a difference in the lives of the kinesthetic whirlwinds in your classroom. In keeping their hands-on busy nature at the forefront, I'm confident you'll do splendidly. May this book help you in your voyage of teaching the must-move-to-learn extra busy kinesthetic child.

Gender Notice

As you read, you will notice that the pronouns regarding the extra busy child switch back and forth. I alternate them for a nonbiased balance in the book.

1

What Makes Extra Busy Kinesthetic Children Tick?

To thoroughly understand the nature of an extra busy child, we need to grapple with the question, what exactly makes an extra busy kinesthetic child tick? The purpose of this chapter is to help you understand a kinesthetic nature and learn how best to reach extra busy children individually through affectionate and meaningful connections. I present a useful questionnaire to aid in discovering a child's unique formula for ticking, as well as methods for calming and redirecting extra busy hands, feet, and mouths in and out of the classroom.

Understanding the Kinesthetic Nature of Extra Busy Children

In today's society an extra busy child's quirks are often frowned upon. Unfortunately, it is common for unusual characteristics of kinesthetic children to be deemed problems, because of the demand for strict classroom management in overcrowded classrooms or to cover up poor parenting.

If you were to look up "kinesthetic" in any dictionary, you would discover that the definition matches the characteristics of an extra busy kinesthetic child fairly well. For example, *Merriam-Webster's Collegiate Dictionary* (11th edition) gives this one: "a sense mediated by receptors located in muscles, tendons, and joints and stimulated by bodily movements and tensions; *also*: sensory experience derived from this sense." Kinesthetic children learn best through movement and benefit from hands-on activities that require it. They are well known for excessive wriggling, fidgeting, tapping their feet, or moving their bodies in other ways when it is deemed inappropriate. Unfortunately, these children are often labeled hyperactive because of their need for continual tactile and physical experiences. These learners excel at athletics, acting, dancing, or any other occupation demanding continual movement.

Our first priority is a child's nature and development. This includes all angles—emotional, cognitive, physical, social—not a set curriculum, schedule, or our convenience. Our second priority is accepting and crafting a lifestyle with routines that nurture our first priority. Our expectations should accommodate and complement the two priorities, not seek to change or cure them. Aside from understanding the above, I recommend being considerate toward a kinesthetic child by accepting the external factors involved: the need for exploration and discovery, and the fact that kinesthetic children exhibit excessive movement.

External Factors

Extra busy children are affected by external factors that powerfully contribute to the direction of their busyness. Here are three significant questions to consider:

Are manageability techniques consistently enforced? Busyness is extra energy. When given proper tools and an individualized plan, extra busy children can excel and channel their extra energy in positive directions. When manageability is not consistently enforced, busyness can quickly get out of control.

Is a support system present? Extra busy children require a loving support system understanding of their nature, personality, and learning preference. They need a support system of parents, teachers, family, and friends willing and able to guide, work as a team, and model appropriate behavior. Without a consistent and stable support system, extra busy children will more than likely flounder.

Is a predictable, sensory-integrated environment in place? Extra busy children need an environment with a sensory-integrated structure, play, routines, consistency, and firm limits. Proper nutrition and adequate sleep are environmental factors as well.

Exploration and Discovery

Speaking from a parental point of view, although only six, Bella holds a PhD in wonderment. Her sense of wonder wasn't taught, rather it was nurtured through self-discovery, exploration, and an extraordinary eagerness to learn. As preschoolers, our first two children enjoyed chasing butterflies, splashing in mud puddles, catching snowflakes on their tongues, and jumping into piles of leaves. But for Bella, her need to explore and to wonder is much more pronounced; it's pressing and probing. She becomes grossly absorbed and oblivious to others during play. Her face and gestures make it obvious that her discovery *gathers* information. Her play *practices* and *carries* it out. It's amazing to observe.

Extra busy children require frequent uninterrupted opportunities for discovery and exploration through open-ended, engaging activities. They learn best when they can re-create experiences and play in their minds with the use of a variety of materials, mediums, and movement.

Excessive Movement

Extra busy children express their desire for skill and play through excessive movement. The kinesthetic children I have worked with best demonstrated productive play when the play was spontaneous, imaginative, unpredictable, and flitting. They had little concern

Busy Bag Trick
Open-ended activities and questions allow extra busy children to expand their thoughts and reasoning as well as look closely at their work. An example of an open-ended question is "How did you make purple flowers with blue and red fingerpaints?" A closed-ended version might be, "Did you use light blue or dark blue for your sky?"

for final products. It was their investigative process and intense physical urge to forge ahead when something didn't make sense that made their nature so kinesthetic. Unfortunately, this must-move-to-learn nature is dampened in most classrooms today, making school cumbersome to the extra busy child.

Kinesthetic Experiences to T.H.I.N.K. About

As a primary special educator, one of the best pieces of extra busy advice I ever received was from a colleague, a veteran teacher I worked with on American Indian reservations in New Mexico. We collaboratively developed Individualized Education Plans for busy children with special needs. She told me, "When dealing with any child's behavior, especially extra busy children, you must stop and T.H.I.N.K." Her acronym taught me to ask myself five important questions that helped me respond effectively to a child's behavior if I deemed it inappropriate or different:

- Is the behavior *true* to the child's nature?
- Am I trying to *help* the child or just attempting a quick fix?
- How will my response *inspire* the child?
- Is a response even *necessary*?
- Is the response *kind* to the child's nature?

Let's break each question down.

Is the behavior *true* to the child's nature? To answer this question it's beneficial to be familiar with the child's personality, learning preference, and possible disability. Does the behavior match up with what you know about the child? Keeping communication with parents open, honest, and objective is very important in answering this question. For the most part, parents know what behavior is normal or not normal for their children.

Am I trying to *help* the child or just attempting a quick fix? At times we are in such a hurry with our own overloaded schedules and deadlines that children receive quick-fix help. Quick-fix behavior modification is seldom helpful. In fact, it's usually a hindrance and not always in the best interest of the child. Here is a scenario to illustrate this question: Beverly's teacher has noted obvious anxiety in Beverly's play the last couple of weeks. She appears nervous and withdrawn. A quick fix for the child's behavior might include medication to alleviate the anxiety. But in fact, it would be in Beverly's best interest in the long run to seek out the root cause of the sudden anxiety.

How will my response *inspire* the child? Will the response encourage or further frustrate the child? The words we select to correct or guide a child's behavior are very powerful. Our reactions can either fuel a fire or put out a small flame.

Is a response even *necessary*? If you understand the child's nature, think carefully about the battles you choose to wage. Choosing your battles wisely is one of the smartest strategies for parenting and teaching an extra busy child. Some things just aren't worth the power struggle. There is very little reason to waste time and energy on no-win situations. Find options within the child's capabilities, and focus on polishing or redirecting behaviors. Leave natural curiosity alone.

Is the response *kind* to the child's nature? If you choose to respond to a child's behavior, always respond in the best interest of the child. Be kind and respectful of her nature while remaining gentle and firm. Your end goal in responding to poor behavior choices should be to make the child aware of the inappropriate actions and the consequences that result from them. Never respond out of anger or frustration.

A Few Extra Busy Stories to Illustrate the Questions

Story 1: Bella loves to draw. She has her own little table for this in our family sitting room. Occasionally, I'll tape large sheets of yellow or orange butcher paper to the wall and let her doodle and draw with her markers on those. Although I cover quite a bit of wall space, her extra busy nature causes her to get carried away. She wanders off the paper and onto the wall. Realizing how much Bella loves this activity—which she does only with *washable* markers—if I notice her veering off the paper, I simply say something like, "Wow, Bella! What a masterpiece! Could you please keep all your special work on the paper?" This gets her refocused and back to work. Nothing else is necessary, except a warm wet washcloth to wipe off the stray markings.

Story 2: Bella's extra busy hands cause many spills—mostly milk, juice, and yogurt. Before giving her these items, I remind her to be nice to her food. This means, don't run with food, wave it around, or set it too close to the edge of the table. When she spills because of one of these careless behaviors, I do not let her have a refill; she may have water. Although some readers may find this somewhat harsh, I do not. I know Bella doesn't want to spill her milk, but she has to eventually learn to control her busyness without continual reminders. A firm response and consistent consequence is necessary.

Story 3: Summer break was over. It was my third day back on the school scene. My self-contained class wasn't large: three boys, two girls. One of the boys, Steve, had autism—high-functioning on the continuum, and extra busy. The first two days with Steve went well. I was getting to know his personality and preferences, and he was becoming aware of mine. This particular morning, however, wasn't so productive. Steve and my educational assistant walked into the classroom. Steve looked directly at my feet, something I picked up on from day one. This time though, instead of putting away his backpack, he began shrieking in terror. I panicked. I hadn't a clue what to do. Approaching him only turned up his volume. My assistant, who had worked with Steve during his prior preschool year nonchalantly voiced, "It's your feet. He can see your toes in those sandals, and your nail polish is chipped. He really hates that."

At first I thought her reply was ridiculous—I couldn't believe such a thing. But soon I discovered it was truthful to Steve's disability.

He did in fact have a fetish for staring at and touching women's feet, and he couldn't stand chipped nail polish adorning them—a *small* detail his parents overlooked sharing with me at registration. I instantly knew such a fixation had to be an extreme social problem. Running up to a woman, dropping down, and touching her feet just isn't acceptable behavior—much less shrieking if her toenail polish is chipped. A lengthy conversation with Steve's mother that evening proved my hypothesis correct. Although it gnawed at me that nothing had been done sooner, an immediate response was necessary, and I initiated one.

Research shows that when children are taught key emotional and social skills, problem behaviors decrease and social skills increase (Joseph and Strain 2003).

Taming Steve's fetish was possible with months of consistent, elaborate strategies matching his nature and emotional, cognitive, and social development. I modeled appropriate actions and redirected his behavior by

- following his lead with his interests continually in mind;
- monitoring the tone and pitch of my voice;
- exaggerating my facial expressions and hand motions;
- picking my battles according to his progress;
- adding drama and make-believe play to situations to emphasize points;
- keeping interactions sensory-integrated;
- teaching in themes (mostly oriented toward feet and toes);
- keeping the environment as calm, pleasant, and positive as possible;
- and teaching social skills, rules, and routines in a sensory-integrated fashion involving
  —sharing,
  —taking turns,
  —asking for something,
  —initiating games with peers,
  —controlling emotions,

—redirecting emotions,

—recognizing triggers, and

—calming down.

I locked in to Steve's academic interests. One of the first things I put into practice was a weekly incentive: classroom-based "feet-time," or time devoted to pedicures. As a class, we massaged our feet with lotion. If earned, the girls could paint their toenails. Whether or not Steve participated depended on his work and behavior for the week. This was both inspirational and enjoyable to Steve.

I also began using "feet-style" teaching techniques. I made feet flash cards with exaggerated toes to teach counting by fives and tens. I used small bottles of nail polish as math manipulatives. I taught sight words centered around feet stories: *The* feet had green socks on them. *My* feet have ten toes. *His* toes are crooked. *All* the toes need to be fresh and clean.

My time with Steve was a memorable nine months. Putting his half-painted-toenail phobia in check while teaching the social inappropriateness of grabbing women's exposed feet was challenging. It would have been unachievable for me had I not taken the time to T.H.I.N.K. and review his emotional and social competencies. Steve taught me to T.H.I.N.K. quickly, preparing me for the following year with Tim, another kindergarten cutie pie you'll meet in chapter 3.

Remember to ask yourself, "Do I T.H.I.N.K. carefully about the extra busy child's nature and emotional/social competencies?"

Questionnaire for Finding an Extra Busy
Kinesthetic Child's Formula for Ticking

The importance of knowing the way an extra busy child absorbs and retains information ranks right up there with the importance of knowing a child's allergies—you just gotta know what a child will or will not react positively to. On the following pages is an in-depth questionnaire I used in graduate school while writing my thesis on sensory-integrated learning. The questionnaire was useful in determining each extra busy student's formula for ticking. It assisted me in looking closely not only at individual preferences but also at my teaching style.

My studies led me to discover that my success in the classroom was directly connected to how informed I was about my students. When I tailored my teaching methods to fit their needs, we were both less stressed, and more successful. Before you complete the questionnaire, I suggest that you look closely at your teaching style by reflecting on your learning style, and ask yourself, "Does my teaching environment cater specifically to *my* learning preference?" If it does, please reconsider it. Remember, your goal is to meet the individual needs of the extra busy child. Knowing the answers to many of the questions will help you more readily apply the ideas and information in *Ants in Their Pants*. I refer to the questionnaire often.

Please carefully consider each question when working with an extra busy child.

How does noise play into the child's nature?

Does he work or learn best in silence, with music playing (if so, what kinds?), with soft sounds, with the TV on, or with others talking? Does he babble or hum as he works? If so, what noises does he make? Do certain situations or places initiate certain unruly noises? Can the child filter out background noise?

What distracts the child?

Is she able to work with visual or physical distractions? Is she able to work near a window or with people moving about? Does she prefer a cluttered space or does her space need to be cleared and well organized?

Where does the child work best?

Does he work best sitting up, with a slant board, in an easy chair, in a beanbag chair, on the floor with a fluffy pillow, at a table or desk? Does he work best with his shoes off or while snacking? Does he move about while working? For example, does he do a few math problems and then move about, returning after a minute or two—flitting, so to speak?

When is the child most alert?

Is morning the best time for the child to work or learn? Afternoon? Evening?

How long will the child focus? (How long is the child's attention span?)

Is she able to concentrate for only a few minutes? A half hour? For long periods of time? Until the project is done? How often does she need to take a break? Is she able to get back to work immediately after a break? Is she able to focus on her areas of interest and also on areas of no interest to her? If there is a gap between the two, how big is it?

Is transitioning from one activity to another problematic?

Does he insist on finishing a task once he's started or can he stop working at any point in the task? Does he like to take breaks in the middle of the task? How does he react to interruptions or being asked to stop midway?

What is the child's working pace?

Is she a fast or slow worker? Is she a piddler or always in a hurry? Does she spend more time (1) getting ready for the activity (clearing the table, arranging crayons just right, making sure she has enough juice), (2) doing the activity, or (3) checking or sharing what she's done?

How do peers affect the child while working?

Does he work best alone or with others? Does he work best in a one-on-one situation? If one-on-one is best, does the other person need to be an adult or older peer? Does he do well in small groups? Large groups? Learning centers?

What kind of structure does the child require?

Is she most comfortable when all task requirements are spelled out clearly and specifically? Does she like to make a few of the choices involved in the task requirements? Does she like to have complete freedom? Does she demand control?

How does the child like to learn?

When learning or playing a new game, would he rather listen to you explain it or see it in pictures? Would he rather read about it or have it read to him? Would he rather watch a video or hear an audiotape? What about watching somebody demonstrate it and then repeating it himself? Does he learn best when explaining it to someone else?

What sort of activities does the child most enjoy?

Which of the following activities help the child learn best?

- reading books or watching videos
- explaining the activity in steps
- discussing the concept together
- playing drill-style games like flash cards
- instructing peers
- fiddling alone
- playing computer games
- going to learning centers
- doing crafts

Do you offer a range of activity levels for the child to experience?

Is the child motivated to learn?

Does she like to show off what she's learned? Does she like to have her work displayed? Does she expect a reward? Does she like to talk about what she's learned as a series of steps or as big-picture conclusions?

What kind of support does the child require?

Does he need incentives or rewards to do a good job? Does he require peer or teacher approval or constant praise and recognition every step of the way? Do tangible rewards need to be in sight? Does he perform well to get attention or does he do it out of intrinsic motivation? Does he work best with a spot lamp on his work? (Spot lamps help children focus. Visit www .thelightshop.com for spot lighting options.)

Consider the following scenario. It is one of my experiences as a regular second grade teacher.

Six-year-old Paul's fidgeting in class was becoming excessive. Paul's father, James, brought him to our conference to discuss strategies for intervention.

When Paul entered the classroom for the conference, he darted straight to our block center and began building towers. At first, James handed him the blocks. This lasted for about four minutes, and then Paul shot over to the art center, plunked himself down on the floor on his stomach, and began drawing with crayons. "Daddy, Daddy! Let's draw together on the floor," Paul suggested, his feet flapping with excitement behind him. Paul made the same request several times. His temper and foot movement increased when his father didn't answer. After about three minutes, Paul's face flushed, his fists clenched the crayons, and an outburst finally ensued. "Daddy! Come draw with me!" At his wit's end, James pleaded, "Paul! Shhh, it's okay! If you'll just calm down, we'll go to Burger King, and you can order anything you want."

I noticed a striking contribution to the problem in those fifteen minutes: at no point during their time together had James really showed an interest in his son's world, one filled with building blocks and coloring on the floor. Paul desperately needed his father to enter his world and give him his undivided attention when he was doing what he enjoyed doing, not what his dad thought he would enjoy. What does the extra busy child in your life enjoy doing?

Just Get Up Close and Personal

I honestly have to wonder how often I have done this with my own children, or students, in the hustle and bustle of each day. How many times have I selfishly looked out for my own interests, ignoring theirs? Many of Bella's tea party invitations have been turned down to the tune of "Not now honey. Maybe after I switch the laundry." Taking the time and effort to step into an extra busy child's world is important for building trust, drawing close, and connecting to her formula for ticking.

As they grow, extra busy children will no doubt face many obstacles related to coping with an extra busy nature in a world that deems it different from the norm. Spending focused time connecting with an extra busy child will lay a firm foundation for a lifelong relationship based on mutual respect, love, and understanding. It will also help him tackle difficulties head-on, with support. Ask yourself, "Do I want the child to confide in me and communicate openly with me? Do I want him to trust me and draw close to me in times of frustration?"

The following pages capture notions that will help you enrich relationships with extra busy children. Use the ideas you like. Tweak them. Share a few from your Busy Bag with someone else. Many are perfect for sharing with your student's parents. Just start connecting!

Make One Thing Your Thing

As parents and educators we are spread extremely thin. We often feel as though we are doling out scraps of our time. After discovering an extra busy child's formula for ticking, plan regular quality time with the child doing one thing that intensely interests her. It doesn't have to be monumental, just meaningful and focused.

A few summers back I taught swimming lessons to preschoolers. To calm their fears in the water I asked random questions. "Do you have a scooter? What color is it?" One bright-eyed, wet eye-lashed natural fish answered my question, "What did you have for breakfast?" with "My daddy makes me waffles from the box every morning. And with chocolate milk." The sparkle in his eyes was priceless.

Where Did You Get That Crooked Toe?

All my children have really crooked toes! This odd physical trait comes from their father. What special feature comes to mind

Strengthening the Home-School Connection

Encourage parents to snuggle up on the couch with a small mirror for quality time well spent with their extra busy child. They can talk about family heritage after giggling over distinguishing traits.

Busy Bag Trick

Hans Christian Andersen's "The Ugly Duckling" is an appropriate story to read if you want to initiate a discussion of ugly, hurting words and actions with extra busy children and their peers.

for an extra busy child you know? Make finding out fun. Standing in front of a large bathroom mirror, identify with the child who he may have inherited his eyes, ears, nose, or any distinct feature from.

"Geek" and "Fatso" Intervention

"Sticks and stones may break my bones, but names will never hurt me!" This childhood escape plea is, well—baloney! Harsh words hurt and often stick forever. As an educator and parent, I have seen how mean children can be to one another. They cut to the core descriptively and quickly. Unfortunately, extra busy children who have a hard time fitting in at school and around the neighborhood can be especially susceptible to cruel jokes, names, and pranks. Do not allow children to torment each other verbally. Intervene!

Walk a Mile in Extra Busy Shoes

To be able to think like a child as an adult is a gift. Even more impressive is being able to walk an understanding mile in their little shoes. Dr. Seuss definitely thought like a child. His work illustrates a child's level of understanding and processing. I'm still mesmerized by Seuss's wonderful stories, full of nonsense words and appropriate humor, and fitting young emergent readers so well. Are you aware of how the extra busy child you influence walks in her shoes throughout the day? What occupies her thoughts? What are her likes? Her dislikes?

A wonderful way to observe an extra busy child's nature is to watch him quietly as he works. What is he doing with his hands? What is he talking about? What is he reading, writing, drawing? I've discovered extra busy children leave subtle and sometimes obvious clues to their behavior. We have to walk in their shoes a time or two to understand them.

Busy Bag Trick
Pump up encouragement or praise by making it open ended. An example of open-ended encouragement is, "Wow! That is an awesome block tower. How did you make it look like the Great Wall of China?" An example of closed-ended encouragement is, "I like your block tower."

Focus with Bulletin Boards

Use a small classroom bulletin board as a shrine for an extra busy child's schoolwork or any other accomplishments. Post good work! Post improved work! Post encouraging self-stick note reminders for the child. Make a child a star for a whole week by displaying pictures of him for everyone to see. Encourage the student's parents to use their refrigerator to display the child's work. They can also use letter magnets for positive affirming phrases: *I LUV U* or *U R AWESOME!*

Recharge

Is it just me, or is it all or nothing with extra busy children? Some days go smoothly and show progress; others are like plodding through thick mud. Whatever kind of day it is, before rounding that corner to the classroom, stop. Take a deep breath. Get ready for what truly matters: the extra busy package eagerly waiting. You know the demanding nature will be active the minute you encounter the child. Prepare yourself mentally.

Busy Bag Trick
To securely store a lost tooth, put it in an old plastic film canister. Wrap it in a small tissue before placing it inside.

Enhance Firsts

Celebrate and enhance first events, such as a lost tooth, with extra busy children. They may forget many things, but your enthusiastic acknowledgment of their firsts won't be among them.

Dare Yourself

An extra busy child's world is much slower than the fast-paced world of adulthood. Three days until a birthday is an eternity! Value can be found in the pace of an extra busy child's life. Chasing a frog or butterfly every once in a while can't possibly be that bad, right? It would probably be good for many adults to try it every so often. Challenge yourself to spend time with an extra busy child. Swing with her, squish your toes in the mud with her, or sit in the classroom with her and do nothing. Merely talk with her. I dare you.

Send Letters Together

My children are blessed with several sets of grandparents. To keep in touch, I purchased photo albums for each set, and together my children and I regularly send items to fill them, including photos, newspaper clippings, special drawings, and cards. Letter writing is a lost art, and it is a wonderful opportunity for one-on-one time with extra busy children. Pick out special stationery for letter writing. Let the child decorate the envelopes. As my children grow, they will either dismiss or continue the letter-writing practice we established. Regardless, their grandparents will have a beautiful memento, and as parents we will have conveyed to our children how much their grandparents should always be a part of their lives.

How Many Kisses Does It Take?

Daily affection can actually boost the immune system. A lot can be gained from touch. A lot can be communicated without it too. Embrace or encourage an extra busy child daily.

At bedtime, Bella loves How Many Kisses Does It Take to Get to Bella's Nose? This game is her special form of affection from her father and me. We start at her fingertips and work our way up her arm. Bella's giggles usually build in intensity as we pass her shoulder, move up her neck to her ear, and finally kiss her chubby cheek and little nose.

Get Out of Your Comfort Zone

The following admission may seem somewhat odd to most, but I accepted my eccentricity long ago. Our middle child, Farrah, is a sensitive gal—remember, a golden retriever personality type with a gentle and soft spirit. At times she struggles with being the middle child. "Bella gets away with everything because she's the youngest, and PJ gets to do more because he's the oldest." To make her feel special, I've given her a unique salutation of affection. Before she darts out the door to school, before bed, and before scrambling off to sporting events, I nuzzle her nose with a light lick—not a slobber, a little lick. It evokes, "You are so gross Mom!" but thereafter intense smiles, especially when Bella demands one. Each of our children has an individualized form of affection. Don't be afraid to get particular with an extra busy child. It'll bring the two of you closer.

When There, Be There

I'm embarrassed to admit this, but when PJ started T-ball, I would take a book to his games. It wasn't until a close girlfriend of mine asked, "So, are you here for PJ or John Grisham?" that I left my books where they belonged—at home. Every minute counts. Extra busy eyes are always watching.

Extra Busy Children Have Dreams Too

Extra busy children are some of the most creative creatures alive. Nurturing and channeling their raw talents in the right direction is important. Placing unrealistic expectations that stem from unmet personal aspirations on extra busy children is unfair, and ultimately detrimental to any relationship. Extra busy children have the right to passionately pursue their interests and dreams with your support.

Adjust Classroom Ties or Family Traditions

All families have traditions that develop over the years. Unfortunately, what worked when an extra busy child was two may not work now that he is seven. Looking at the values and reasoning behind customs is important, especially as extra busy children grow and siblings are welcomed into the family. It's also important to properly inform relatives, fellow child care colleagues, or teachers of a child's extra busy tendencies so that everyone is on the same page.

Although it sounds harsh, it's probably not worth it to have relatives or educators who don't accept an extra busy child's nature—making it obvious through blame, unsupportive accusations, or frustration—around the child. One parent I worked with said,

"As a family we just stayed to our own. We were tired of our own flesh and blood not understanding. It's hard to see your child ridiculed and laughed at. They just rolled their eyes. Who needs that? We didn't. Our kid didn't either."

Incorporate Classroom or Family Meetings

It is highly recommended that families and classes of young children sit and eat together regularly. If this is not an option, try sitting at the table for a ten- to fifteen-minute group conference to discuss, vent, and grapple with issues of importance. Here are some examples from my family and classroom meetings:

> "I've asked Farrah over and over to knock before she barges into my room, but she's not doing it!"
> "We have a field trip tomorrow. Let's discuss our rules for field trips again."
> "Mom, I'd like to talk about my chores. I think I have too many."

While we as parents and teachers have the final word at home or in the classroom, we may in fact find ourselves in a family or classroom conference negotiating, or admitting, "You made a good point. Let me think on it, and I will get back to you."

Sharing meals or holding regular classroom or family meetings allows everyone a chance to vent and express themselves. These meetings model the use of healthy conversation that keeps communication lines open. Do not make the meetings optional. Guidelines need to be clearly defined before every meeting. Common guidelines include the following:

- Only one person speaks at a time.
- No name calling.
- Meetings must be planned and announced in advance.

Use Free Entertainment

Taking the time to play simple games like Hopscotch, Ring Around the Rosie, Tag, Hide and Seek, London Bridge, and Follow the Leader can naturally draw extra busy children close to you. And simultaneously, they ignite one of nature's best medicines—laughter.

The following are free forms of playful entertainment to enjoy together with extra busy children. Use them in your classroom and share them with parents.

Play I Spy. Spy colors, objects, or words.

Play charades. Animal Charades is the best! Make it easy and humorous for small extra busy children by pretending to squirm like a worm, waddle like a duck, or jump like a kangaroo.

Invent magic tricks together. Teach a child the Pepper Run trick. Get a dish of warm water and sprinkle pepper into it. Have a child dip his finger in dish soap and then in the center of the dish of water and pepper. Watch the pepper scram to the sides. Play up the tricks with a top hat, cape, and magic wand.

Visit a fire station. Ask for a tour. You may have to call ahead and schedule a time.

Put on a treasure or scavenger hunt. Make creative visual maps for the hunt.

Visit a museum. Most children's museums have wonderful hands-on exhibits.

Take a walk and talk. Put on your tennis shoes and head out the door with a small baggie for collecting things. Play games while you walk. Who can find the weirdest looking stick? Who can find the coolest looking rock? Who can find the biggest leaf?

Make a kite and fly it together. With the child, see if you can make a contraption that will actually fly. Paper sack kites are simple.

Have a play picnic inside. Spread out an old sheet, make sandwiches, and play simple card games.

Visit a pet store. Check out the hamsters, fish, reptiles, and puppies with a child.

Visit a construction site. Sit in a vehicle with the child and watch huge cranes, cement trucks, or jack hammers at work. Discuss their different uses.

Volunteer together. Call a local animal shelter, church, or food bank. Offer your time.

Pull out coloring books and crayons. Bella, Farrah, and I love to have coloring contests with scented markers every now and then.

Make popcorn and go through old photo albums. If your photos are in boxes like many of mine, sit together and fill the albums.

Camp out inside. Pull out sleeping bags and flashlights and tell stories.

Once an extra busy child experiences the power of playful affection and comfortable connection with you, he'll attempt more of it and look forward to squeezing it in anytime. So what are you waiting for? Start connecting!

Below are two final ideas for connecting I couldn't resist sharing. Toss them in a monthly newsletter home to parents.

Put Up Your Jukes! Children benefit from play, especially good-natured physical play with the adults in their lives. Thumb and arm wrestling are good examples. Not only are they exciting, they are effective strategies for connecting and helping to release busy energy. In our home, wrestling is a blast. When PJ was around two, I recall my husband getting on his knees next to him, poking his little tummy, and light-heartedly saying, "Put up your dukes son!" PJ, in turn, squealed, "Put up my jukes!" Two children later, this has evolved into what our family calls "juking." PJ and Farrah enjoy an occasional round, but Bella loves regular rounds.

These are usually induced by her flopping on the floor, spreading her arms out wide, and giggling, "Mom, come juke me!" Five minutes of juking ensue when I get on the floor and attack her cheeks with kisses. "No kisses for sale today!" she announces, trying to get away. I lightly restrain her, giving her neck a big wet raspberry kiss. "Ooh Mom! Gross!" she giggles. I nestle my nose in her ear, sneak an "I love you" in it too, and continue rolling back and forth with her wrapped in my arms.

Like any game, playful wrestling for connecting should have rules. Here are five we follow:

- Safety first.
- Focus on playful affection.
- Don't overpower a child.
- Stop when someone says stop.
- No tickling allowed. Not everyone likes being tickled.

- **Mommy Makeovers.** Bella loves to brush my hair and clip it up with fancy barrettes and bows. She loves to "make me into a princess" with old makeup. Extra busy little girls (and boys) can hone fine motor skills while dressing Mommy up with lip gloss, blush, and eye shadow. A mommy makeover is a wonderful time for connecting through heartfelt dialogue. I make sure to have lots of wet wipes nearby for cleaning up and a hand mirror to use while praising Bella for "making me beautiful." Fill a basket with accessories like costume rings, clip-on earrings, or sparkling diamond tiaras to enhance a mommy makeover.

Calming Extra Busy Bees

Extra busy children can be a handful, especially when busyness sets in. The following points are helpful to remember for effectively quieting kinesthetic busy habits and behavior in and out of the classroom:

- **Keep the atmosphere positive.**

  Extra busy children demand and crave attention. When speaking to them, watch the tone of your voice. Smile even when speaking firmly to the child. Positively redirect off-task busy behaviors. Give lots of hugs and kisses and praise too.

- **Keep your responses prompt.**

  Extra busy children are often on focused missions. Every question is vital. Every reply counts. Whether a pressing question or behavior needing immediate quieting or redirecting, your response should be prompt.

- **Keep things simple.**

  An extra busy child's life should be kept as simple and consistent as possible. Rushing through or stuffing an extra busy child's day with unnecessary distractions and expectations is a recipe for disaster.

- **Keep consequences clear.**

  Extra busy children require clear choices and consistent consequences for their actions. Consequences from Monday should apply on Wednesday. Changes of any sort should be specific and presented to the extra busy child as soon as possible.

Ways to Calm Extra Busy Children

The following are more than thirty strategies to add to your Busy Bag. They will be helpful when extra busy trials unfold. Share them with parents, especially the last eight.

Washcloth Wipe Down: The combination of heat, hunger, and fatigue can call up intense crankiness in young extra busy children. Gently wiping a child's face with a cool cloth can be calming. In the winter, use a warm one.

This Little Piggy: To calm an extra busy child almost anywhere, peel off her sweaty socks and shoes and play This Little Piggy. Teach her the nursery rhyme as you wiggle one toe at a time, starting with her big toe.

This little piggy went to market.
This little piggy stayed home.
This little piggy had roast beef.
This little piggy had none.
This little piggy cried "wee, wee, wee" all the way home.

Music: Fussy children engrossed in extra busy habits can often be appeased with gentle music accompanied with rocking, swaying, or swinging. Nature sounds, Baroque music, and compositions by Mozart are calming.

Fabric Rubbing: Give a cranky kinesthetic child a pocket-sized piece of silk, satin, or velvet to fidget with while out and about doing errands. Larger pieces can be used as blankets for swaddling or cuddling while rocking.

Deep Breathing: After having three children, I comprehend the power of deep breathing to relax. Teach an extra busy child to breathe deeply, in through his nose and out through his mouth, when irritated. Add arm motions: arms up while breathing in, arms down while breathing out. Initiate deep breathing together when you notice the child becoming angry or frustrated.

Pretend Play: Extra busy girls and boys can be eased through bothersome busyness by acting out situations using dolls. "Rolanda, how about you be the curly-haired doll, and I'll be the red-haired doll. Let's talk about recess today. You did not want to come inside when recess was over; you threw a fit. Is there anything you would like to talk about?"

The Burrito Roll: I worked with young extra busy autistic children for years. When wound up, they could be calmed with a few burrito rolls. Spread a medium-sized fluffy blanket out in an open space on the floor. Have the child lie at one end of the blanket, with his head outside the blanket, and proceed to roll him up like a burrito. Once again, make sure his head is always outside the blanket. When tightly rolled up, ask, "Is my stuffed burrito ready to roll?" Then gently roll the child out.

Hair and Forehead Stroking: Another effective way I soothed extra busy autistic students was stroking their foreheads and hair back gently. Bella enjoys this while "reading" picture books to me.

Honing Peripheral Vision: Having eyes in the back of your head can alleviate many oncoming extra busy incidents. Children who think you actually do have eyes in the back of your head aren't as likely to act out. Regularly use your peripheral vision while working with extra busy children. Practice cutting negative behaviors off at the pass.

Lights Out: This is a common classroom quieting technique, but it can also work with small children who are throwing an extra busy fit. Turning off the lights can get a child's attention long enough to redirect their behavior, especially if the room turns pitch black. Bella and I have stood in a dark bedroom many times while I review her bedtime routine. "Bella, playing dolls is not a part of your bedtime routine."

Rocking: Rocking chairs can be a lifesaver. Rhythmic rocking with soft music can alleviate irritability in small children. I recommend that every teacher have one in her room for extra busy children to take rocking breaks in.

Animal Promises: Critters have a unique way of motivating children to listen and learn. Keep a class pet or incorporate incentive- or reward-based animal outings for an extra busy child. Bella loves to feed ducks at a local park. Petting zoos or pet shop visits are worthwhile too. Use the time to focus on behavior.

"LeShannon, you will scare the ducks if you are too noisy. Let's feed them quietly. Watch me."

"Courtney, the little goat needs to be stroked gently. Can you stroke the goat gently? Like this."

"Adam, you will scare the fish if you tap on the aquarium glass. Let's quietly watch the fish. Do you see the clown fish?"

The Back Scratch: Bella loves it when I lightly scratch her back. This is especially effective when she is tired or short-tempered. I have her lie down flat on her tummy, and then I scratch her back in rotating motions—small circles, big circles, up and down, sideways, and in zigzags. Softly rubbing velvet, satin, or silk fabric on her back calms her down too.

Holding, Swaddling, and Cuddling: Some people believe that excessive holding of small children will spoil them. But when my children or primary students are obviously frustrated or upset, a hug often comforts them. Also, I never allowed my children to cry for long periods of time as toddlers. Children cry for a reason.

Leaving the Scene: When an extra busy child throws a tantrum, move to another area of the classroom. If he follows, ignore him. Dramatic tantrums often require an attentive audience. He will probably give up when he notices that you aren't paying attention or that his fellow classmates are looking at him oddly.

Singing: Sometimes when I want to get my point across or gain a student's attention, I sing my words. I use a familiar tune such as "Baa Baa Black Sheep."

Giving the Look: My husband has more luck with this quieting tool. If Bella's noise level rises, he'll give her The Look—a raised eyebrow, one closed eye, and a stare. The Look can also be used in the classroom, but should never include a frown or mean facial expression. Here are five steps to help you give The Look:

1. Stare at the student, not angrily, but stare. This step may be enough. You might be able to stop right here.
2. Move well into the student's personal space, bend down to her level and very quietly, so that only she can hear, say her name.
3. Then tell her exactly what you want her to do or stop doing.
4. Then thank her, again saying her name.
5. Move out of her personal space.

(adapted from Wong and Wong 2001)

Speaking Calmly and Clearly: Yelling is a very ineffective strategy for calming extra busy children or stopping or redirecting busy behavior. Always try to remain calm. Stand your ground and calmly express yourself repeatedly: "Charley, you may not go to centers until you finish your work. Charley, you may not . . ." Keep your instructions to a direct statement, not a request. Repeat in the same tone, as needed. Over and over and over.

Work the Busyness Out: If the child isn't being terribly wild, just his busy self, and he is not hurting anything or anyone, ignore him. Let him do what he does best—be about his busyness.

Reminding about Rules: When my kindergarten students were not motivated to do their seat work or cooperate, I would remind them of the class rules and the consequences for choosing not to follow them. "Sasha if you choose not to do your work now during work time, then you will have to finish it during learning center time. Which do you choose?" Follow through with the consequences of their choices.

Getting a Chill Chair: A time-out chair can easily acquire negative connotations. When a child needs a break to refocus or calm herself down, send her to the chill chair. Our chill chair is a huge brown recliner, dubbed Snuffy. The big chair engulfs Bella. It is useful when I am finishing something in the kitchen or on the phone and Bella needs to cool her jets for a minute or two. I point to Snuffy and say, "Go chill, Bella."

Having Patience: Bella often makes a mess of her books. She tends to scatter them all over the floor during the course of an afternoon of use. When I ask her to clean up the books, she does—only in her six-year-old extra busy way. The books are stacked on the shelf sideways, upside down, and sticking out every which way.

When you ask a child to do something and he responds appropriately in conduct and effort, yet not completely up to task, be thankful. Progress is always praiseworthy. Honestly, I appreciate the scattered books; they demonstrate an interest. Don't expect quieting or redirecting miracles overnight.

Giggling: Use a knock-knock joke or two to stop a blooming extra busy behavior or episode.

"Knock knock, Ian."

"Who's there?"

"Orange."

"Orange who?"

"Orange you glad you kept your feet off the table? Good choice!"

Warm Clothes: Clothes that are just out of the dryer are fabulous for snuggling. When Bella is having a hard time cooperating with dressing in the morning, I warm her clothes up in the dryer for five to ten minutes. Her spirit is lifted, and she becomes eager to cooperate after I nuzzle her in them.

Riding around the Block: A ride around the block a few times can
- calm an extra busy child,
- refocus a disobeying extra busy child, or
- put an overly tired busy child to sleep.

Leaving the Radio Off: Instead, play soft ocean or woodland sounds. Baroque music and compositions by Mozart are also suitable suggestions.

Warm Baths: I've yet to meet a child who doesn't enjoy a warm bath. Use a warm bath as an incentive at the end of the day. "Ming, if you finish picking up your room, you can take an extra bubbly tubby."

Aromatherapy Massage: Eucalyptus, rosemary, and lavender oils can relax children when used for tender massaging. Warm up the oil, pour it into your hands, and gently rub the child's tummy, back, or chest. Bella enjoys having her neck rubbed too. Keep the oil away from the child's eyes.

Ceiling Fans: This one was passed on to me by a girlfriend. Spread a comforter out underneath a whirling ceiling fan, lie down with the extra busy child, and sing to her. Tell her a story. Ask her to tell you a story. Many children find ceiling fans mesmerizing and calming.

Do Nothing—Really: When a child is hungry and exhausted from a long day in the sun or an especially trying day at school, simply feed him and put him to bed. Not much else can be done. The combination of fatigue and an empty tummy can produce unbecoming behavior in children.

Big Bear Hug: To calm an out of control child, dole out a huge, all-encompassing bear hug. Hold the child snugly, sway back and forth, sing, and talk to her.

No More Messing Around: If you have warned an extra busy child to stop a behavior, like throwing rocks, and he chooses to continue, intervene by physically stopping him and removing him from the situation. As stated before, be calm but firm. If at the park, sit in the car with the child. If at the grocery store, leave. If at a restaurant, take the child to the restroom. Stick to the bottom line: you are in charge, and certain behaviors are not allowed—period.

In Closing . . .

Before we head into chapter 2, quickly revisit the quotation from Maria Montessori that opens this chapter. Remember, children are like snowflakes; no two are alike. They each have their own unique nature and way of ticking. Consider the questionnaire and each extra busy child's social and emotional competencies when planning your weekly lessons. Sometimes it's the little details that determine the pace and *grace* of a day. Something as simple as an enthusiastic high five or cheerful smile the morning after a difficult day can be a monumental help for connection, change, and setting the scene for a more encouraging day. And don't forget: *the main thing is to keep the main thing the main thing*. The children in the classroom are the main thing!

For further ideas, games, and activities to T.H.I.N.K. about regarding an extra busy rabble rouser, check out these resources:

- *Celebrating Young Children and Their Teachers* by Mimi Brodsky Chenfeld (2007)
- *Daily Preschool Experiences for Learners at Every Level* by Kay Hastings, Cathy Clemons, and April Montgomery (2008)
- *Take Time to See through Children's Eyes,* CD (2007)

All three are terrific additions to your Busy Bag. Suggest them to your students' parents too.

2

An Extra Busy Child's Best Environment

Dimensions Educational Research Foundation has found that many of today's classroom environments are either over- or understimulated (Rosenow 2005, 1). Both environments are difficult for an extra busy child to function within. An overstimulated child care or classroom environment often displays toys piled high, cluttered play spaces, constant unnecessary noise, and walls covered in pointless posters or outdated student work. The environment may be unorganized. Procedures may be unfocused. Assessment is sometimes inconsistent. Children are easily distracted, and the atmosphere is at times chaotic. On the other hand, an understimulated child care or classroom environment is often geared toward one learning preference, uses the same play materials over and over, seldom engages in outdoor activities, and may be more concerned about disciplining children than encouraging their learning process. Class routines can be lifeless. Children aren't always challenged, and the atmosphere is dry.

A kinesthetic child's learning environment should be sensory-integrated, attractive, orderly, and purposefully arranged. It should welcome learning. An extra busy child will benefit from a learning environment in which

- Environmental materials are stimulating, simple, and regularly rotated to keep children motivated and interested.
- The teacher demonstrates a love for learning. An educator's sense of wonder and excitement to learn is apparent, encouraging, and motivating to children.
- There are opportunities for a lot of contact with the outdoors for both structured activities and unstructured play.
- Children take regular and safe movement breaks and engage in activities that cater to a kinesthetic nature.
- A predictable schedule with clearly defined, discussed, and modeled procedures is followed.
- Assessment is varied and student directed. Student work is displayed and changed often.
- The needs and interests of the kinesthetic children match the environment.
- All areas of childhood development are promoted: physical, social, emotional, cognitive, aesthetic, and linguistic.
- Play of all types is offered.

This chapter discusses possibilities for an extra busy child's best environment and explains how to productively meet environmental needs for a kinesthetic learner.

Developmentally Appropriate Practice

Extra busy children who enjoy going to school are naturally more productive in the classroom and less likely to unleash busy habits than are children who dread going to school. Certain classroom practices are developmentally appropriate for kinesthetic children. With such practices in place, the child will be more likely to feel excited about going to school.

The National Association for the Education of Young Children emphasizes guidelines for developmentally appropriate practice, otherwise known as DAP. Organizations such as the National

Association of State Boards of Education and the National Association of Elementary School Principals stand by their resources and recommend implementing the guidelines below for preparing and carrying out high-quality programs for young children (Kostelnik 1993). The guidelines cater wonderfully to an extra busy child.

What exactly is developmentally appropriate classroom practice? Three basic principles define and prove its effectiveness for helping children learn.

1. Developmentally appropriate means taking into account everything we know about how children develop and learn and matching that to the content and strategies planned for educating them in early childhood programs.
2. Developmentally appropriate means treating children as individuals, not as a cohort group.
3. Developmentally appropriate means treating children with respect— recognizing children's changing capabilities and having faith in their capacity to develop and learn.

(Kostelnik 1993, 2)

I have found that turning these principles into questions is helpful for lesson planning and pondering educational intervention strategies for extra busy children. Ask yourself

- Is this lesson or strategy in keeping with what I know about child development and learning?
- Does this lesson or strategy take into account the extra busy child's individual needs?
- Does this lesson or strategy demonstrate respect for the extra busy child?

Working with extra busy children is a one-day-at-a-time endeavor, thus, the importance of a Busy Bag. One of the most wonderful features of DAP is its natural placement of children on a continuum of learning. You can guide them from point to point as new skills and behaviors are acquired. I've discovered that in following DAP guidelines I eliminate a considerable amount of unnecessary and wasted time, energy, and work.

An Extra Busy Developmentally Appropriate Environment

An extra busy child's environment requires developmentally appropriate practice. To meet this demand, I suggest the following ten instructional strategies:

1. Provide ample time daily for active exploration, discovery, and wonderment indoors and out.
2. Allow regular times for free play, especially constructive play.
3. Incorporate simple learning centers.
4. Provide several ways to approach a task (using multiple intelligences).
5. Model a passion for learning. Guide, rather than dictate, instruction and hold students accountable for their learning process. Encourage parents to model appropriate and desired behaviors.
6. Teach thematically (across the curriculum).
7. Sing a lot.
8. Sensory integrate your teaching approach and delivery methods. (Remember, not all children learn the same way.) Use activities that motivate the child. Examples include songs, fingerplays, puppets, prompts, flannelboards, games, books, and effective encouragement.
9. Keep activities extremely open-ended and engaging.
10. Use a system of student self-directed assessment. (Make students aware of their strengths and weaknesses.)

Extra Appropriate Classroom Tools and Techniques

Extra busy children will benefit from being taught tools and techniques for redirecting their natural busyness during times of intensity. A helpful technique for home and school is helping the child to directly grasp and understand more about himself and how he can ultimately control and manage his own behavior with support. Checklists and reminders are fabulous tools for initiating such support. Make the child a resourceful and creative checklist with pointers for dealing with his extra busy habits throughout the day. For nonreading children, use pictures. Laminate the lists. Turn several into a small booklet. Send classroom copies home to parents. A sample list might include the following pointers:

Hi Rowan,
At school today, remember to . . .
✓ Try not to sit next to friends who talk to you or bother you.
✓ Work on only one assignment at a time.
✓ Keep your eyes on your teacher.
✓ Keep your fidget toy quiet.

Effective teachers are effective role models and leaders. Lead extra busy children to discover their best selves using developmentally appropriate classroom practice. Do not leave them to wonder or wish the day away engrossed in anything else.

Additional DAP Resources

Developmentally Appropriate Practice in Early Childhood Programs Serving Children from Birth through Age 8 by C. Copple and S. Bredekamp, eds. (2009)

Successfully Moving toward Developmentally Appropriate Practice: It Takes Time and Effort! by J. L. Vander Wilt and V. Monroe (1998)

The Power of a Predictable Schedule

A predictable schedule with routines is one of the easiest ways to accommodate an extra busy child's environmental needs for learning and increase her behavioral success rate. A predictable schedule can significantly refine extra busy habits and spare many headaches in the classroom and at home. A predictable schedule can work effectively for an extra busy child if

- The classroom is set up to match the schedule.
- The schedule is properly established and modeled.
- The schedule is consistent and sensory integrated.

Because extra busy children are wired for movement, patterns and signals help keep their must-move-to-learn nature within boundaries and limits. Knowing what to expect each day enables extra busy children to focus more on their learning process and behavior and less on what will or will not *get them in trouble*. A predictable schedule for an extra busy child in and out of the classroom should include the following elements:

- **An enthusiastic morning greeting**

  Every morning, greet the child with an uplifting affirmation or effective praise, such as "Happy Tuesday, Penny! Are you ready for a fun day at school?" and "Earl, you did such a wonderful job listening yesterday. I know you can do it again!" Stand at the door of your classroom with open arms and a big smile.

  For an enthusiastic morning greeting at home, wake the child with affection. I wake Bella by kissing her cheeks and whispering in her ear, "Wake up, Sleepyhead! Morning came early."

- **A morning presentation of the day's events**

  Create and post a visual one-task-at-a-time schedule for the child. Verbally go over the schedule with the child daily, possibly first thing in the morning with breakfast, or during morning circle time in the classroom. The schedule should be posted in the same spot each day.

- **Connecting points in the schedule**

  Extra busy children thrive with mental connections. For example, snack is eaten *only* at the table. Seatwork is done *only* in the morning. Completed homework is placed *only* in the blue box. Backpacks are hung *only* on a designated hook in the classroom. The same can exist at home for connecting points:

Dinner is at 6:00 PM, after soccer practice. Bath time is always after dinner.

- **Consistent modeling of the schedule**

  Help an extra busy child listen to and follow directions by modeling appropriate technique, behavior, and application of the schedule.

- **Sensory integration of the schedule**

  Lock into a child's formula for success by following posted predictable routines. Use vibrant hand gestures, sign language, and creative visual cues to enhance the schedule. You might sing to transition or use hand puppets or fingerplays to begin a new activity.

- **Clearly defined procedures**

  In *The First Days of School*, education experts Harry K. Wong and Rosemary T. Wong state, "The number one problem in the classroom is not discipline; it is the lack of procedures and routines" (2001, 167). Clearly defined procedures make daily routines flow. Extra busy children will not function well in a classroom if procedures are unorganized or chaotic. I recommend clearly discussing and demonstrating procedures for

  —entering the classroom and putting her backpack away;

  —getting the teacher's attention;

  —sharpening her pencil and having her work collected;

  —entering the classroom if she is late;

  —gaining permission to use the restroom;

  —lining up;

  —getting ready for lunch, recess, and going home.

  Share the following information with parents: Clearly defined procedures are just as pertinent at home. I recommend that extra busy children have routines at home with clearly defined procedures for

  —getting ready for school,

  —doing homework,

  —participating at dinnertime, and

  —getting ready for bed.

  Please share with parents the Bedtime Check-Off Card found in appendix B.

- **Regular movement breaks**

  An extra busy child's schedule requires regular movement breaks. Take the breaks as a class or individually. Here are three quick classroom ideas:

  —In the morning, schedule the child to take the attendance card to the office or the lunch count to the cafeteria.

  —In the afternoon, have the child walk to the school library for a storybook intentionally left with the librarian.

  —Before dismissal, let the child pass out papers or reorganize the bookshelf.

- **An enthusiastic end of the day**

  Close the day enthusiastically, even if the day didn't run as smoothly as you'd hoped. Help the child gather his supplies. Stand by the classroom door as the child exits. Give him an end-of-the-day hug or high-five with "See you tomorrow!" Enthusiasm is contagious, even at the end of the day. A regular bedtime routine should close each day. I discuss bedtime routines in more depth in chapter 6.

- **Daily celebrations of behavioral and academic successes**

  Squeeze these in whenever you can. Consider every moment a possible teaching, redirecting, or praising moment. Effective encouragement at the end of one day will go a long way toward setting the stage for the next.

Classroom Tools and Techniques

Along with consistency and predictability, the organization of an extra busy child's environment has tremendous influence on redirecting or eliminating extra busy habits. A sensory-integrated organizational approach, using as many of the senses as possible or effectively pairing senses, is a highly productive tool for organizing an extra busy child's environment. Examples of paired senses include

- manipulating playdough to practice letter names and sounds (visual, tactile, and auditory);

- testing the buoyancy of items in a large tub of water while discussing sinking and floating (visual, tactile, and auditory);
- listening to an interactive storybook on tape with a peer, or working on a computer with a combined task like following along in a book (visual, tactile, and auditory).

I have found the following sensory-integrated organizational techniques especially helpful for structuring an environment for kinesthetically natured children:

- **Clearly label the environment with words, pictures, and/or concrete objects.**

  Clearly label the items or areas an extra busy child uses regularly. Make sure students are aware of proper placement for items and maintain the area's order. Label bins for toys or manipulatives. Use pictures in place of words for nonreading small children.

- **Structure student work areas.**

  Whether a child is working at a desk or a table, keep the area structured.

  Look at the picture on this page. Courtney has a bucket for all her supplies. She has a task folder outlining her morning activities. Her journal is placed below her task folder for easy access. Notice the clock, picture, and

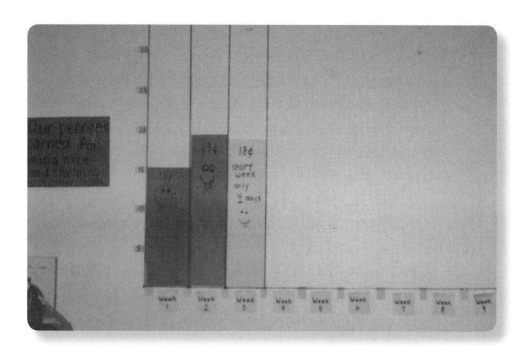

written words immediately informing Courtney that she will visit the occupational therapist at 12:30 today. Although a transitioning tool, it assists Courtney in having a successfully structured school day. The same train of structuring thought can be carried to the home environment, where the child does homework or reads. Suggest that parents designate a homework or a reading spot that is not in front of the TV. Make sure the child has a container of supplies readily available to keep her from wasting time searching for a pencil.

- **Engross extra busy children in their learning process.**
  Allow students to regularly display their work and other evidence of their progress around their desks and in the halls. Suggest to parents that they display their child's work around their home as well. This encourages participation, self-confidence, and responsibility for being a part of a learning or home environment striving for excellence. The photograph on this page shows a weekly tracking chart for student progress, an excellent example of displayed student accountability for learning.

- **Incorporate an incentive program that is tangible, visual, and consistently reinforced.**
  Clearly define an incentive-based behavior management program with a system of rewards and consequences for

Ten fabulous classroom incentives extra busy children enjoy:

- Hugs, high fives, affirmations
- Free play time at a learning center of choice
- Extended recess
- Show and tell
- Being the line leader
- A healthy edible treat (bananas, apples, crackers)
- Something from a well-stocked treasure box
- Being first—at anything!
- A no-homework night
- Computer time with a favorite program

good and poor behavior. Here is a description of an effective incentive program I used in my classroom.

After surveying my students' interests, I filled a huge fish tank with price-labeled prizes—15 cents for a cool folder, or 25 cents for a stuffed gorilla. All of the children decorated a baby food jar that would hold their penny earnings for working hard, cooperating, listening, and following class rules throughout the week. The jars were very effective for getting a child's attention—coins being added for good choices or sometimes being taken out for poor ones. I would purposely clang and rattle the jars for praise and pennies earned for good choices. "Courtney, wow! You earned three more pennies for listening so well." I would dramatically take three pennies from the big penny jar and one by one let them clink in her jar while giving effective praise.

I would pull the student aside for consequences and pennies lost for poor choices. "Courtney, you chose not to line up for recess when told to do so. I'm sorry, but your choice lost you two pennies." At the end of the week students could purchase prizes from the toy tank with their penny earnings. This incentive program worked well because of its sensory-integrated approach. It can be used on the home front as well.

- **Clearly define and sensory integrate classroom procedures**. Sensory-integrated classroom procedures work best for extra busy children when demonstrated daily. Try to keep the procedures simple, yet versatile and creative. In my kindergarten special needs classroom I used a sensory-integrated line-up system. I tied colored flags to a long white nylon rope. Each child received a daily number corresponding with a daily color. I posted the child's name by the number and color, and when called to line up, the child would have to locate her spot. The hand-held rope line-up system was helpful for extra busy movers who tended to wander off as we progressed down the hallway.

- **Implement a system of student-directed assessment**. Portfolios are a form of assessment that allows teachers or

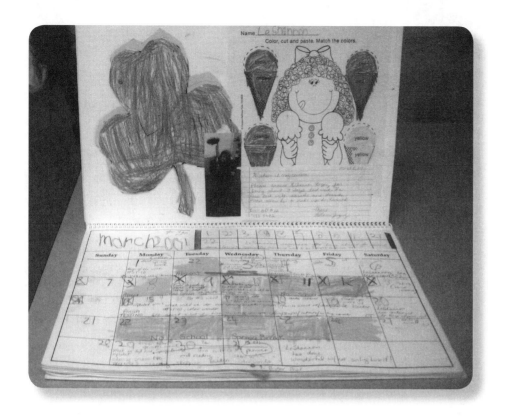

parents to gather work samples and anecdotal notes over time to assess a child's academic growth and overall development. It is beneficial to let older extra busy students direct their portfolios for accountability and self-confidence purposes. Portfolios can become a showcase of student work and progress that a child will eagerly want to share. I discuss portfolios and anecdotal notes in detail in chapter 3.

Extra Tool Tidbits

Keeping a kinesthetic extra busy learner actively engaged in any environment can be tricky and trying at times. The following ideas can prove helpful for nurturing a must-move-to-learn environment:

- **Time activities appropriately.**

  Whatever the activity, keep it in a time-appropriate context. An extra busy child will fade or fidget if environmental activities are drawn out or too short.

- **Alternate activities regularly.**

  Switch senses and techniques regularly. For example, if you are studying the ocean in language arts, read books to the children about the ocean. Have them pair up and read books to each other, or take them to the school library to check out books on their own. Let them decorate pages of written vocabulary words from a story. In short, use a variety of learning modes to keep the extra busy child interested and motivated.

- **Use theme activities periodically.**

  Many educators, myself included, love to teach thematically. Extra busy children benefit tremendously from thematic units, even at home. A classroom example might include a unit on bears: Read "Goldilocks and the Three Bears" and then role-play the story (language arts). Learn about the foods bears eat and what they do in the winter (science). Have the children make books about bears or write collaborative stories about bears (writing). Brainstorm differences between real bears and teddy bears. Let students bring in teddy bears for show and tell. Discuss how bears live. Draw and research caves. Take a field trip to a zoo to observe live bears. The ideas are endless.

  For variety, plan theme days in accordance with holidays, special events, or the curriculum. For example, have a pajama day, crazy hair day, crazy sock day, all red day, or slippers day.

  Inform parents of home theme ideas to reinforce all sorts of academic and social skills. For example, Bella's grandparents took her to Disneyland when she was five. Before she went, we looked up pictures of Disneyland. We read about Disneyland online and mapped out how long it would take to get there. We discussed necessary behavior at Disneyland—so many strangers! We talked about the food she would probably enjoy. We colored pictures of Disney characters and watched Disney movies to prepare her for the trip.

- **Evaluate the environment frequently.**

  I suggest that all educators and parents stand at the front of their classroom or front door and ask, "Does this environment look inviting? Is it organized or cluttered? Is it brightly lit and clean or dirty and dim?" Believe it or not, lighting and layout do affect learning and a child's ability to remain mentally engaged. I try for a simple layout that is not distracting. Even the smell of an environment can encourage or discourage participation. When teaching, I regularly took my bread machine to school and started baking the bread in the morning for an incentive snack in the afternoon. It made our classroom smell divine— the entire school wing, in fact!

Nurturing a must-move-to-learn environment can make all the difference in an extra busy child's daily behavior and learning process. Use your imagination, network, and lock into student formulas to get the ball moving in the right direction.

In Closing . . .

Before moving on to chapter 3, remember this: any child's learning environment, especially a kinesthetic child's, should creatively beckon "Come play! Come explore! Check me out!" And don't forget the importance of consistent and predictable schedules. When sprinkled with inspiration, both consistency and predictability help extra busy children thrive. Through teaching experiences, I have discovered that it's those little rote routines that keep busy bees on task and focused throughout the day. Regularly reinforce proper classroom procedures; they result in successful school days for extra busy children.

For further reading regarding an extra busy child's best environmental needs and how to productively meet them, check out these resources:

Designs for Living and Learning: Transforming Early Childhood Environments by Deb Curtis and Margie Carter (2003)
A Study of Early Childhood Program Environments CD-ROM by Deb Curtis and Margie Carter (2006)

Both resources will help you greatly enhance your classroom environment and Busy Bag. Be sure to strengthen the home-school connection by suggesting the books to your students' parents.

3

Working with Extra Busy Children

This chapter presents and discusses productive ideas for working
with extra busy kinesthetic children in and out of the classroom.
It outlines the power behind simple sign language and discusses
the benefits of effective transitioning, redirecting, and behavioral
logging.

When working with naturally kinesthetic children, the following
ideas should be implemented for the children to learn effectively:

- Play both indoors and outdoors.
- Work in short blocks of time rather than long ones.
- Take frequent movement breaks.
- Provide as many sensory-integrated learning opportunities as
  possible.
- Build and construct things.
- Use memory techniques requiring movement, like hand
  gestures, sign language, or mnemonic devices.
- Use flash cards, checklists, and color-coded items when
  possible.
- Allow lying on the floor with lots of pillows when studying,
  enabling feet to move.
- Express feelings through physical movement like role-playing.

- Communicate with hand gestures.
- Provide reading materials that are brief, bold, or summarized.

The Power of Sign Language

Foreign-language teachers have suggested that learning a second language helps students think beyond the confines of their own culture (Wilcox and Wilcox 1997). I first became intrigued with using sign language to propel my students while I was teaching in a multi-impaired classroom. I was researching sensory-integrated learning strategies for my master's thesis and discovered that signing with children, both hearing impaired and not, had endless benefits—not merely those promoting verbal language. "Children love multisensory learning that involves seeing, hearing, speaking, and doing. Sign language can enhance language experiences by engaging all of these modalities. Teaching sign language is a developmentally appropriate practice that promotes acceptance of differences and allows for hands-on language learning in the early years" (Good, Feekes, and Shawd 1993, 81). Using sign language with children

- promotes sensory-integrated teaching and learning;
- helps children focus, listen, and pay attention;
- promotes better understanding of others with special needs;
- enriches and adds excitement to the classroom; and
- promotes learning through multiple intelligences.

Dr. Gayle Hosek-Spies, a diagnostician for the Farmington Municipal School District in Farmington, New Mexico, and cochair of my graduate studies committee, expressed that teaching sign language to children who are not hearing impaired can be very advantageous. It develops preverbal and overall communication skills. In addition, it can be effective for expressing feelings and even assist in taming behavior.

Signing Experiences Inside and Outside the Classroom

My teaching in a multi-impaired classroom incorporated signing as a method of sensory-enhanced communication. Basic signs were stapled to many of my students' individual education plans. Having the children learn basic sign language became necessary, and one can't effectively teach what one doesn't know, right?

While taking a crash course in sign language, I didn't reinvent the wheel, but turned to the Baby Signs program developed by Linda Acredolo and Susan Goodwyn. The Baby Signs program doesn't use formal sign language. Instead, it stresses the natural signs babies and children already use, encouraging their use of signing along with spoken words (Shapiro 2003, 49). This concept was especially helpful for the extra busy children with special needs I worked with, primarily those with Down syndrome and severe ADHD. I moved on to more advanced American Sign Language (ASL) as time went on.

The Baby Signs program (www.babysigns.com) is a must for Busy Bags. *Sign with Your Baby* by Joseph Garcia is also a great investment. Garcia's signing approach (based on ASL) is slightly different from Acredola and Goodwyn's, but it stresses the same overall goal: enhancing communication with children.

It's never too late to begin signing with extra busy children. Bella knows about twenty-five basic signs, which I've found especially helpful when out and about, running errands, or visiting relatives. Simply signing "no," "stop," or "car" helps busy Bella transition during times of difficulty, like leaving swimming sessions. For example, if I know we will be leaving our swimming session in, say, thirty minutes, I catch Bella's attention and sign "car" (by pretending my hands are on a steering wheel and moving them back and forth as if driving). I then point to the big clock on the wall. Twenty minutes before departure, I swim over to her, get directly in her little face, make eye contact, and sign the gestures again, adding words.

"Bella, we are leaving in twenty minutes." Ten minutes before leaving, I do the same thing. Five minutes before leaving, I repeat it again. When it is time to go, I help Bella stop and transition. This routine is similar to the one I carried out in my multi-impaired classroom, except I used timers and visual cue cards.

Teaching an extra busy child basic sign language can prove advantageous, especially when it comes to expressing feelings, boosting communication skills, and transitioning from one activity to the next with ease.

Suggestions for Getting Started

- Learn how to make a sign or create one on your own and show it at every opportunity. Consistency is key. Try not to get bent out of shape if the child doesn't make the sign perfectly. Praise his effort.
- Be sure to speak the word clearly with the sign.
- For younger extra busy children, move the child's hands to make the sign the first few times. If the child seems receptive, continue. Never force it.
- Start with the child's most pressing needs and interests. We started with "book" and "banana," two of Bella's favorite items.
- Encourage everyone in the classroom to follow along with the signing. You'll often notice younger children trying hard to keep up with older siblings or classmates. Learning from them can be easy—and essential—for extra busy children.
- If implementing signing in the classroom, educate parents about it. I always made a mini dictionary of the signs we were working on for my students' parents. I posted signs as wall charts too.
- Use as many signs as possible throughout the day. Remember, you don't limit your spoken words. A child will pick up signs at her own pace. Add signs liberally.
- Keep in mind that learning sign language with children who are not hearing impaired is educational and can boost self-esteem.

- Keep it pleasurable. Even if you do it for a brief period of time, an extra busy child will benefit tremendously.

The following pages present the signs I used in my multi-impaired, self-contained kindergarten classroom. I start with the basic ASL alphabet. Sign language often requires using the basic alphabet to initiate more advanced signs. Look at the sign for "eat" on the next page; O sign, fingers toward mouth, tap on lips. Do you see how knowing the proper ASL O sign beforehand comes in handy?

You can adapt signing techniques from the Baby Signs program or basic ASL, whichever you prefer. Remember, perfect technique isn't necessary for extra busy children who are *hearing*.

Alphabet List

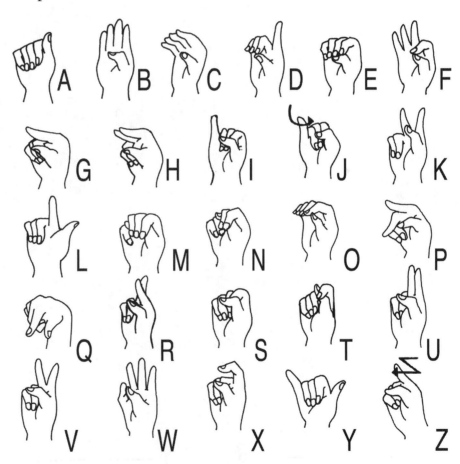

A Simple Starting Sign Language Word List

Apple  Make an X hand and twist it in your right
cheek.

Ball  Tap fingertips of both open hands,
making a circle.

Banana 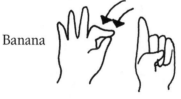 Hold up your left index finger
(representing the banana), then use
your right-hand fingers to go around
the left finger pulling off the peel.

Book 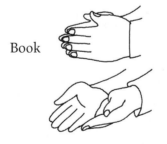 Place your hands palms together,
then open and close hands with little
fingers as the spine of the book.

Eat  Tap your O hand, palm down, on your lips.

Happy   Tap your chest with an open right hand, palm facing body, in an upward motion.

Hello   Wave back and forth with an open hand (also means good-bye).

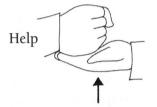

Help   Close your right hand and rest it on your left open palm, then lift both hands together.

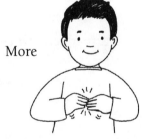

More   Hold both hands with fingers together and palms facing each other, then tap fingertips together.

No   Tap your right index and middle fingers and your thumb together.

Play  Hold both hands in Y shape, then lightly twist them back and forth.

Please  Make a circular motion on your chest with your open right hand.

Stop  Hold both hands open with your right hand little finger down and your left palm upturned; your right hand cuts down to end on your upturned left palm.

Thank you  Hold your right hand flat with all four fingers to the lips, then move your hand a few inches forward.

Basic Colors

Children pick up on colors quickly. Teach extra busy children visualization cues with color signs. Get creative by using props to enhance colors signs. Two examples are

- squeezing a small orange ball in one hand while signing "orange" with the other;
- jingling a small yellow band of bells in one hand while signing "yellow" with the other.

Black  Draw a line across your forehead, from left to right, with your right index finger.

Blue  Make the B hand, then twist it back and forth.

Brown  Slide the B hand down the side of your right cheek.

Green  Make the G hand, then twist it back and forth.

Orange  Hold your C hand at your mouth, then open and close it.

Purple  Make the P hand, then twist it back and forth.

Red  Draw your right index finger down across your lips.

White  Hold an open hand on your chest, then pull out and close to the O hand.

Yellow   Make the Y hand, then twist it back and forth.

Additional Sign Language Resources

Signing for Kids by Mickey Flodin (1991)

A Show of Hands: Say It in Sign Language by Mary Beth Sullivan and Linda Bourke (1980)

The Joy of Signing: The Illustrated Guide for Mastering Sign Language and the Manual Alphabet, 2nd edition, by Lottie L. Riekhof (1987)

Signs for Me: Basic Sign Language Vocabulary for Children by Ben Bahan and Joe Dannis (1990)

Sign to Learn: American Sign Language in the Early Childhood Classroom by Kirsten Dennis and Tressa Azpiri (2005)

Transitioning Ideas

Extra busy children often have difficulty transitioning or moving from one activity to another. They often become engrossed in their exploration and discovery, and really can't shut down and shift gears without help. I have found the following ideas helpful for extra busy children experiencing difficulty transitioning:

- **Allow enough time**.

  Always allow extra busy children enough time to move from one activity to another. For example, Sarah visits the school occupational therapist three times a week at 1:30 in the afternoon. At 1:10, Sarah's teacher informs her that in twenty minutes she will be going to OT. At 1:20, her teacher walks over to her desk, looks directly at her, and states, "Sarah, you will be leaving for OT in five minutes." (The remaining five minutes are for transitioning and walking to the therapist's room.) When it is time to go, Sarah's teacher helps her stop what she is doing and transition.

- **Give warnings**.

  Extra busy children benefit from continual reminders before transitioning, especially during interesting outdoor play. I'm sure we could all swap horror stories about pulling a child away from the playground. Use time-marking verbal reminders along with sign language as suggested earlier in this chapter. Here are some common verbal reminders for transitions.

  —"One, two, three, eyes on me!"

  —"Ready, set, look!"

  —"Pencils up!"

  —"One, two, three, listen and see!"

- **Give cues**.

  Simple transitioning cues may include flashing the lights on and off or bringing out Sparky, a cute stuffed puppy who gives directions for activity changes. Additionally, visual cue cards make helpful transitioning tools. Do2learn is a Web site specializing in free and commerical teaching resources for pupils with learning difficulties. The site is also very useful for educators looking to enhance their teaching strategies. Do2learn offers pictures on its Web site, www.Do2learn .com, that you can print out and use for cueing and making schedules. If the child has a daily task chart, have her remove the picture when the task is complete. Remember, extra busy children thrive on consistent, predictable schedules. I strongly recommend a daily, visually cued schedule for extra busy children to help with transitioning.

- **Use timers**.

  When a child starts an activity, set a timer nearby, preferably in sight. Walk by and tap the timer at ten minutes before transitioning and again at five minutes before transitioning. The final bing signals that time is up. Help the child transition.

- **Use prompts**.

  Verbal, visual, and physical prompts cater well not only to overall skill acquisition but also to transitioning. I once worked with an extra busy child who had Down syndrome. She was having trouble going from swinging to lining up when recess was over. I developed a strategy for helping her that used colored bandanas, an interest of hers. I waved a green bandana as we walked outside together. This meant, "It's time to swing!" Fifteen minutes into her twenty-five-minute swinging session, I flew a yellow one high above my head directly before her. This meant, "Swinging time is almost up!" The last, a waving red bandana, meant, "Swinging is over. Time to line up!" This transitioning prompt, along with the incentive of earning the privilege of waving all three bandanas as we walked inside, worked well for this student.

- **Use games to teach transitioning**.

  Here's an example for a game I call Ready, Set, Move. Lay out five activities separately on a playground, lawn, or open area indoors. Possibilities include a jump rope, a simple puzzle, two dolls, a Hula-hoop, and a kick ball. Have the child start at the first activity, and direct him to move after five minutes. Make sure to warn him with, "Ready, set, move." Start with five-minute intervals and gradually reduce them to thirty seconds.

  A catwalk is another alluring transition tool. Use colored masking tape to create an amusing catwalk from one activity to the next. Make one long balance beam line from the block center to the computer center for the child to walk along. Make the catwalk zigzag, wind, or spiral. Change the child's transitioning catwalk every other day. Before transitioning, announce, "Five minutes until we walk and meow on the catwalk!"

- **Grab the child's attention**.

  Baiting a child's attention, especially by using her interests, can effectively aid in transitioning from one activity to the next.

Here are some catchy ideas to creatively grab a child's attention for transitioning purposes:

—Initiate a short fingerplay or song, preferably one the child has never heard.

—Say, "Nicholas, I have something in my pocket. Let's talk about what it could be as we clean up and get ready for lunch."

—Show the child an interesting picture. Initiate transitioning or another activity, like cleaning up, as you talk about it.

—Put on a fancy hat and ask, "Do you like my hat?"

—Pretend to put on special tiptoe shoes or magical earmuffs during transitioning times.

—Ask the child if she would like to pretend to ride a magic carpet to the next activity.

—Change your voice. Make it crotchety or silly as you initiate transitioning.

—Use a sock puppet or story mitt to initiate a change in activity. A colored funny face on the end of a tongue depressor stick is a simple and quick idea.

Busy Bag Trick

I recommend avoiding abrupt transitions. Unfortunately, the need for sudden changes does occur. For these times, I've found swaying my body and clapping to a familiar rhythm while transitioning with kinesthetic children works exceptionally well. Start with loud clapping and gradually clap at a softer level.

Redirecting Extra Energy

Knowing an extra busy child's preferred energy zone is important for redirecting, substituting, and zoning busy behavior. Let me briefly define "preferred energy zone" and "zoning busy behavior" to ensure we stay on the same page.

A child's "preferred energy zone" is the part of his body that releases excess energy. Most kinesthetic children exhibit energy zones of busy hands, feet, and/or mouths. The phrase "zoning busy behavior" denotes bringing the preferred energy zone under control with direct support and the child's awareness.

You want to lock into the child's formula for ticking to find new ways to release extra energy in a positive direction. Please realize that your ability to manage a child's busy behavior largely depends on whether you maintain a calm demeanor. Productively redirecting, substituting, or zoning a child's unnecessary behavior will be next to impossible if you are irritated, frustrated, or feeling downright incompetent. I've been there and done that!

Knowing a child's preferred energy zone and maintaining a calm demeanor play a major part in redirecting, substituting, and zoning extra busy energy.

Let me share a personal tidbit, which I elaborate on in chapter 6, to bring the concept a little closer to home. I struggled for many years with an eating disorder. Unfortunately, by the time I finally sought help, my poor eating habits and destructive behaviors had become so ingrained, a part of who I was and how I functioned, that I had to literally learn to eat all over again. This was only possible through redirecting, substituting, and zoning of my poor eating behaviors, which allowed for new ones to keep me healthy and productive as a parent and teacher. The following three anecdotes provide examples of redirecting, substituting, and zoning:

Redirecting: A formal definition of "redirecting" might sound something like "the process of making the child aware of her unacceptable behavior and immediately showing or modeling a behavior that is acceptable." Here is an example: In my multi-impaired classroom, I encountered a kindergarten boy with autism who spent a considerable amount of time making loud animal noises—an extremely distracting habit. To redirect the behavior, I would walk over to him with a coloring page of the animal he was imitating (I kept a file folder containing his regular animals on my desk), put it directly before him, and present him with three crayons in my palm. The noises stopped as he selected a crayon and then began coloring the animal picture. Oddly, his little feet would begin tapping intensely. Such shifting was easily mitigated with a carpet wedge under his desk. This redirection activity worked well for this child.

Substituting: To substitute means to replace or stand in for. Here's an example of substituting: Anxiety was a major factor in my unhealthy eating habits. I'd get nervous and start nibbling on anything and everything in sight to soothe myself, preferably my nonstop hands. I learned to substitute this unhealthy habit with a better one: swinging on playground swings. We live four houses down from a playground. To this day, when I feel myself getting overly anxious, Bella and I walk the short distance to the park and take advantage of the sturdy swings.

Zoning: Zoning is slightly different from redirecting and substituting. The goal of zoning a child's busy behavior is to make the child distinctly aware of it, allowing her to work on controlling it. Here's a sample zoning activity for a child who has extra busy hands. It should clarify the differences.

Juanita is having difficulty keeping her hands to herself at the playdough learning center. She continues to grab at and take her playmates' play materials without asking or sharing. To zone Juanita's hands, offer her a pair of medical or food-service gloves to manipulate the playdough. The goal of this activity is to help her become aware of using words, not aggressive hand movements, to express her needs. Model and demonstrate the process of asking to share another child's playdough in front of Juanita while you are wearing the gloves. Let other children have a pair if a request is made. This activity slightly disenables the hands, making the child aware of unnecessary hand habits. The gloves are *not meant as a humiliation tactic.* When progress is shown, an incentive or reward should accompany the task: "Good job, Juanita. Did you know, for twenty minutes, you asked to share the playdough before just taking it? Your good hand choices earned five minutes of extra free time!"

Ideas for Redirecting, Substituting, and Zoning Busy Hands, Feet, and Mouths

Busyness, the language of kinesthetic children, can be expressed through busy hands, busy feet, and busy mouths.

Listed below are strategies I've found helpful for redirecting, substituting, and zoning the three busy areas. Most are fitting for redirection or substitution and can be creatively zoned according to a child's individual needs. Remember age appropriateness when choosing activities; not all activities are appropriate for all ages. Also, some of the exercises are more enjoyable than others. If you want to make a stronger point, use an activity less thrilling to the child.

Busy Hands

Bella's preferred busy energy zone is her hands. She constantly engages in excessive hand movement: hitting, slapping, tapping, flicking, and knocking things over. These are helpful strategies for redirecting busy hands:

- Give the child a Koosh ball, pom-pom ball, Nerf ball, or small piece of fuzzy material to put in her pocket to squeeze or stroke.
- Have the busy child fold washcloths (new terry cloth ones work well) or small remnants of velvet.
- Let the child play with some of the goopy, gooey substances listed in chapter 5.
- Let the child pop bubble wrap.
- Let the child play with a Slinky.
- Let the child hammer golf tees into Styrofoam with a small plastic hammer.
- Give the child a large sponge to squeeze or pinch.
- Give the child a plastic bowl full of small, colorful rubber bands to sort by color on her fingers.
- Give the child a can of mixed nuts to sort out into cups. (If the child is allergic to nuts, disregard.)
- Give the child a bowl of peanuts to shell and sort (If the child is allergic to nuts, disregard.)
- Have the child use link and chain toys that snap together.
- Help the child use lotion to massage her hands and arms.
- Show the child how to plant annuals in a flower bed. Demonstrate planting one annual. Let her plant several using only her hands, not gardening tools.
- Give the child an old cell phone to practice reciting and calling pertinent phone numbers, such as home, grandparents, cell phone numbers, and emergency numbers.

- Give the child a vegetable peeler or hand-held grater and a carrot or potato. Demonstrate proper use of the utensil to keep the child from cutting himself—remember to scrape away from, not toward yourself.
- Give the child a piece of sandpaper and a small block of wood. Have her sand the wood block for five minutes.
- Have the child husk ears of corn, shell peas, or tear fresh, wet lettuce—awesome sensory activities.
- Fill a sink with water and dish soap bubbles. Let the child clean toys in it.
- Give the child a big container of rice, beans, or birdseed to put through a funnel or dig through. Hide small toys inside the container.
- Let the child do simple puzzles (preferably eight to ten pieces).
- Sit with the child. Have him close his eyes while you draw shapes on the back of his hand. Have him try to guess the shape.
- Give the child an old shoe without laces. Hand her string, yarn, or laces to lace the shoe.
- Give the child a newspaper to tear up. Request certain shapes or a designated number of torn pieces. Have him clean up the shredded pieces when done.
- Therapro, Inc. offers a dressing cube with different fasteners on each side, including tying, fastening Velcro, buttoning, zipping, and buckling. All are perfect for occupying busy hands (www.theraproducts.com).
- Have the child close her eyes. Give her an object and ask her to feel and identify it.

Busy Feet

Kinesthetic children with extra busy feet constantly tap, shake, rock, swing, kick, or stomp their feet and/or legs. Before listing suggestions for managing this zone, I would like to share a quick tidbit. Kinesthetic children with busy feet often benefit from straddling their chairs horseback-style while working. Such seating gives their chair more stability and controls foot movement. These are helpful strategies for redirecting busy feet:

- Have the child wear socks that single out each toe. Fuzzy, oversized socks work well too.
- Give the child a small blanket to wrap around himself while doing schoolwork or reading.
- During naptime, put a strip of fuzzy material at the end of the child's mat to tickle his toes on.
- Take the child outside with a footbag. Kick it around with her.
- Let the child jump on a mini trampoline or swivel in an old office chair.
- Tape bubble wrap to the floor and encourage the child to try to pop each bubble individually with his toes.
- Have the child close her eyes. Give her an object and ask her to feel and identify it.
- Purchase a wobbling plastic punching bag. Let the child kick and punch it vigorously.
- Put a yard or two of colored masking tape down on the floor or carpet. Have the child remove his shoes and walk the line back and forth on his tippy toes. Have him put his arms in the air to make the activity more challenging.

Busy Bag Trick

Children with busy feet often do not do well waiting in line at a teacher's desk. I suggest placing a waiting chair next to your desk. Post a rule: "If somebody is in this chair, you have to stay in your seat until this chair is empty." Also, give kinesthetic children a laminated list of waiting options, such as

You may fidget with your fidget toy.

Check the odd-numbered problems on your paper.

Draw on the back of your paper.

Busy Mouths

Extra busy children with energetic mouths, especially strong-willed ones, tend to try to get the last word or argue after boundaries and rules have been well established. Extra busy mouths can also unleash odd and unruly noises. These are helpful strategies for redirecting busy mouths:

- Give the child a straw, some celery, or a carrot to chew on for five minutes or so. Other gnawing items include a frozen banana, toothbrush, or frozen bagel.
- Give the child a glass of water with a straw to blow water bubbles.
- Let the child blow bubbles or blow up balloons. Please remember age appropriateness and safety at all times with balloons.

- Take the child outside with a whistle. Blow one with her.
- Give the child a piece of gum and have him chew it for five minutes without talking. Let him time himself with a timer.
- Give the child ice chips to suck on.
- Have the child brush her teeth with a vibrating toothbrush.
- Have the child lie down on the carpet, or clean floor, and instruct him to do fifteen indoor snow angels while singing a movement song (see chapter 5 for movement songs).
- Give the child an oversized calculator and age-appropriate math facts on paper sheets. Have her recite the problems out loud as she uses the calculator to solve them.

Using Humor for Busy Mouth Redirection

Humor is an effective tool for redirecting and substituting extra busy habits. Here are several fun and light-hearted ideas for redirecting boisterous or unruly noises:

- Redirect a busy mouth with "Kori-Ann would you like to do a few tricks with me? They are lots of fun!"
  - —*Trick one:* Face the child and hold hands. Together, attempt to turn inside out by swinging your arms over each other's head and completely back around to the front again. See how many times you can turn around without letting go of each other's hands.
  - —*Trick two:* Sit on the floor with the child and link arms back to back. Together, try to stand up without letting go.
  - —*Trick three:* With the child, lie down on the floor and touch feet (heads at opposite ends). Try to roll across the floor without disconnecting your feet.
- If a child is being too loud, model a softer level. Of course, if she is making inappropriate noises, initiate a different sound. For example, you might teach her to whistle or to do a hand jive with accompanying bebop sounds.
- Tongue twisters such as "She sells seashells by the seashore" and "Peter Piper picked a peck of pickled peppers" are entertaining. You can also make up your own.

- Louis R. Franzini, author of *Kids Who Laugh* (2002), suggests playing the Ha Ha game. To play, the first person says, "ha"; the second person says, "ha ha"; the third person says, "ha ha ha"; and so forth. This game is sure to shift annoying noises to laughter.
- Use exaggerations. For example, start a sentence and let the child finish it. "My doll was so big that . . ." "The neighbor's dog was so crazy that . . ."
- *Mr. Brown Can Moo! Can You?* by Dr. Seuss is a book of wonderful noises. Initiate a few noises from the book.

Ideas for Any Zone

A great idea for controlling busyness in single-file classroom lines is to let the extra busy child be at either the front of the line or the back of the line and have a designated job, such as turning off the lights or walking three steps in front, as if to clear the way. Be creative and perceptive. Distract an extra busy bee, and remove temptations whenever possible (objects, peers). The goal is to prevent potential busy incidents. Remember, an ounce of prevention is worth a pound of cure.

Listed below are several additional ideas for redirecting a busy mouth, hands, or feet:
- Sort or ball up colored socks.
- Sort crayons, tossing out the old ones.
- Straighten a bookshelf.
- Dust tables with a big feather duster.
- Sweep the floor.
- Pass out papers.
- Wipe tabletops with a clean, wet rag or wet wipes.
- Rake leaves, pull weeds, or shovel snow, depending on the season.
- Water potted plants or a garden.

Mary Poppins used a spoonful of sugar to make unpalatable tasks enjoyable. Do the same for redirecting extra busy energy, keeping in mind that extra busy children are trying to make sense of their world through excessive hand, foot, and mouth movements. Make sure the extra busy child understands it is only his extra busy behavior you disapprove of at times. I'm convinced that if they could articulately express themselves, they'd more than likely say

"I don't mean to be so ornery."

"I really do want to focus better."

"I can't help being so noisy."

Logging Busy Behavior

Using anecdotal notes and portfolios, two effective discovery and assessment tools, became important to me while I was teaching extra busy kindergarten children with special needs. Logging daily observations of them engaged in play and class work became a valuable tool. I tapped into small details and formula insights by logging observations of what I saw and heard in my classroom. I eventually brought my logging techniques to the home front with Bella.

Luckily, logging isn't limited to behavioral intervention. Logging is effective for documenting cognitive, language, social, emotional, and physical development as well, all of which can aid in uncovering extra busy behavioral situations.

I commented earlier on a kinesthetic-natured boy with autism named Tim. Tim taught me about the power and simplicity of using anecdotal notes and portfolios to assess extra busy behavior and learning. Let me share my logging lessons from Tim.

I encountered Tim for the first time in the school counselor's room. He was lying on the floor, tummy down, one eye open, one closed, and strategically lining up toys. "Hi Tim," I said, bending down to greet him. Tim only grunted at me, not once removing his fervent focus from the toys. "Tim really likes things just so," his grandmother told me.

Tim proved to like many things just so. Most problematic was removing all his clothes to use the restroom. Tim had a tight and demanding procedure for doing so, one he didn't like interrupted.

1. While sitting at his desk, Tim would remove his shoes, then socks, folding and placing one sock inside each shoe.
2. Tim would proceed to the restroom and continue systematically removing all his clothes, folding each item, and placing it on top of the others in a very orderly fashion outside the stall door.
3. Tim would use the restroom then work in reverse order to become fully dressed again.

The entire procedure lasted twenty to twenty-five minutes. It was very distracting, very interrupting, and very unnecessary. The behavior needed to be redirected immediately. I had a conference with Tim's grandmother, and we decided to begin attacking the problem together in steps by logging his behavior through anecdotal notes and the use of a portfolio.

Anecdotal Notes

Anecdotal note taking is evaluation that allows educators to document the progress of a student by observing the child while he is engaged in daily classroom activities. Anecdotal notes can be used at home by parents too. Anecdotal notes include the child's name, date, and a narrative of what the teacher or parent sees or hears during a selected time. Anecdotal notes are records of individual incidents that incorporate specific quotes, descriptions of interactions with other children, or noteworthy skill performance. They are not based on opinions; they are statements about observable behavior. Anecdotal notes record events that happen as children interact with their environments. They can guide planning and instruction for extra busy children. Anecdotal notes work effectively if the following four questions are answered carefully:

- **What system will you use?**
  Some teachers log notes on index cards, others use a notebook. At home I use a spreadsheet, but in the classroom I use a small calendar. A blank calendar form can be found in appendix B. Decide which will be the most convenient method for consistent logging.
  When working with Tim, I scribbled down my notes in a notebook during the school day and then transposed them onto

a portfolio calendar to share with his grandmother at regularly scheduled conferences.

When we're away from home, I log Bella's anecdotal notes in a small loose-leaf notebook that fits perfectly in my purse or in a side pocket of her Keep 'Em Busy bag, which is a bag of simple, quick, novel activities that can entertain a kinesthetic child while limited in tight quarters. Limited spaces for extra busy children may include a rehearsal room for a spring music program, a long school picture line in a crowded gymnasium, or a dentist's crowded waiting room. There's more about Keep 'Em Busy bags in chapter 4.

- **What are you looking to observe and document?**
  Remember to keep documentation concrete and objective. I suggest using a code. You can make up your own creative system.
  DD= daydreamed
  WH= worked hard
  TF= threw a fit
  DT= didn't transition
  TW= transitioned well
  WA=wandered around

- **How often will you be looking at your notes?**
  Anecdotal notes can quickly become lengthy, especially if you are tracking the behaviors of more than one student. I recommend looking over your notes weekly. A week is enough time to see patterns develop. Summarize what you have observed in a statement at the end of the week to send home to parents or to discuss during a scheduled conference at the end of the month. More pressing behaviors like Tim's, however, may require shorter frames of time.

- **What's your next move?**
  After reading the gathered notes, it's time to hypothesize. Use anecdotal notes to attempt problem solving. Put on your sleuth's hat. Let's look at some sample anecdotal notes to illustrate the process.

Student observation, October 11, 9:45 AM:

Adela put one block on top of another. "I'm making it tall, Mrs. Cross." She continued stacking blocks, commenting on the tower's height and how it was becoming almost as tall as her. "Look! Look! I did it, Mrs. Cross!"

Follow-up comments:

Adela is becoming more confident in her abilities. She is not asking for as much help.

Student observation, October 19, 8:15 AM, arrival time:

Frank ran into the classroom and threw himself down on the rug, disregarding all normal, structured activities. He screamed to his father, "Don't leave me! I hate Mrs. Cross! She is mean. I hate school!" I asked his father to leave, expressing that it would be best and reassuring him that I'd call him. Frank continued to yell, "Come back!" He lay down on the rug and continued sobbing for about ten minutes. When he stopped crying, I approached him and positively asked if he'd like to join us. He said, "Yes."

Follow-up comments:

Although I was absent the prior day, Frank had a good day after his initial fit in the morning. This is becoming a pattern; I am noting that he doesn't do well with substitute teachers. I will need to prepare Frank for my absence when possible.

> **Observation of Bella, June 20, 9:20 PM:**
>
> Bella was put to bed later than usual tonight. Phil was umpiring, and we stayed to watch him. She ate half of a hot dog from the concession stand. She finished her Keep 'Em Busy bag snack. At the game, Bella ran up and down the bleacher stairs with a few other kids. She interacted well. I didn't have to break anything up.
>
> **Follow-up comments:**
>
> Bella didn't swell from the hot dog and wasn't grumpy the next morning. She does so well behaviorally after a good swim.

If anecdotal notes are taken regularly and correctly, they can provide valuable feedback regarding a child's progress. They can assist you in narrowing down situational busy behaviors over time. There are three steps in anecdotal note taking:

1. Identify and specifically define the problem.
2. Collect information to determine the behavior's function.
3. Categorize the behavior and form a hypothesis about why it is occurring.

Using daily anecdotal notes ultimately aided in ceasing Tim's problematic bathroom ritual. Let's look at each step and how it assisted in addressing Tim's behavior.

Step 1: Identify and Specifically Define the Problem

During step 1, it is necessary to pin down the behavior that is causing the learning or discipline problem and define the problem in concrete terms that are easy to communicate, facilitate record keeping, and measure progress. Vagueness in logging will cause confusion. Use specific definitions.

- Vague: "Tim is aggressive when not allowed to carry out his obsessive bathroom ritual."

- More specific: "Tim hits other students and throws items that are on his desk when frustrated over not being allowed to carry out his bathroom ritual."

When collecting specific descriptions of the behavior, it is pertinent to take the following into account:

- Expectations: Are your expectations for the child too high or too low, resulting in frustration, fear, or embarrassment on the child's part?
- Culture, religion, and home language: Knowing what children bring to the classroom from home is very important. On the American Indian reservations in New Mexico, the culture and religion are different from mine, so discussing cultural differences with Tim's grandmother was necessary for ruling out certain possibilities. Make sure to address the differences right away.
- Various settings: Although Tim's behavior was bathroom oriented, speaking with caregivers, past teachers, and his grandmother helped to identify specific characteristics of the ritual and determine if the ritual existed when Tim was in the care of others.

Step 2: Collect Information to Determine the Behavior's Function

Step 2 of anecdotal logging is predicting when, where, with whom, and under what conditions the behavior is most likely or least likely to occur. The following are questions I used when working with Tim (and Bella) to gather information about extra busy habits and behaviors:

- When is the behavior occurring or not occurring? Is there a specific time?
- Where exactly is the behavior occurring?
- Are there certain triggers for the behavior? (Other students or siblings can be triggers, for example.) What are the events before or after the behavior? Could a trigger be weather, testing, field trips, parties, or TV shows? It's important to leave no stone unturned.

- Do cause-and-effect conditions exist? When A occurs does B always occur? For example, when Bella eats pizza in a restaurant her fingers and hands swell, and she becomes crabby.

Step 3: Categorize the Behavior and Form a Hypothesis about Why It Is Occurring

The purpose of anecdotal note logging is to find the most effective way to address and redirect a persistent problematic or detrimental behavior that is holding a child back from her full potential. Once you have specifically defined the behavior—having gathered information about when, where, and how it happens—you are ready to tackle the reason for it, the why. In forming a hypothesis of why, you must begin asking yourself questions. I find the following questions helpful:

- Is the child engaging in the behavior to gain attention, stimulation, escape, or control something in the environment?
- Is the child's inability to perform a specific skill or task due to developmental delays or is a lack of formal instruction propelling the behavior?
- Is the child's lack of motivation due to poor self-esteem, an understimulated environment, or some unknown variable?

After forming a hypothesis, you can begin redirecting or eliminating the behavior. Here is the hypothesis I formed for Tim: Tim's restroom ritual appears not to be merely for bodily functions. Tim demands to go to the restroom and carry out his obsessive ritual during times of transitioning to social activities like recess or lunchtime. Logging suggests that as environmental stressors build up, Tim uses his ritual as a way to escape. His grandmother has noted that he does periodically use the restroom *normally* at home. The function of Tim's ritual appears to be to avoid interaction with other peers. The behavior seems to be functional and motivational. A skill deficit does not exist.

Busy Bag Trick

Motivation comes from two sources: extrinsic and intrinsic. Motivation is extrinsic when external factors are the primary influence on an extra busy child's learning. For example, a child sits quietly, listening to a story for twenty minutes, only because he connects cooperating to receiving a reward. Intrinsic motivation, however, comes from within. The child sits quietly, enthralled by an interactive storyteller, longing for just one more story! Enjoyment and passion for what is occurring in his environment are motivating him. It is important to encourage intrinsic motivation in extra busy children.

Portfolios

A portfolio is a form of assessment that uses work samples gathered over time to analyze and note student progress. I use portfolios to showcase a child's work—including his strengths and growth—not merely to track weaknesses. I used a portfolio while working on Tim's disruptive bathroom ritual, and I accented his strengths in it. I find three questions helpful for portfolio assessment:

- **What will you use as your portfolio?**
  Some teachers prefer a sectioned notebook or tabbed folder. I find calendars and journals useful. I rely on products from Bare Books, which has a complete listing of portfolio possibilities on its Web site, www.barebooks.com.

- **What will go inside?**
  I fill portfolios with pictures, crafts, paintings, drawings, writing samples, and rubrics. Although more fitting for an anecdotal log, I often include brief narratives about social interactions, physical changes, and development of fine and gross motor skills with selected portfolio pieces.

- **How and when will you schedule conferences with parents?**
  I schedule conferences for extra busy children with special needs every four weeks. This works well for me. I've seen educators evaluate and have conferences every six or nine weeks. Personally, I find nine weeks too long of a time period between evaluation periods. Six weeks may be suitable if the child is in good academic standing. I do not suggest using e-mail or doing phone conferences. Portfolios are a visual assessment tool, preferably directed and shared by the child. Experience has demonstrated to me that student-led portfolio conferences instill confidence, responsibility, and accountability in extra busy children. The extra busy child wants to produce a beautiful portfolio to show parents or caregivers and say,

  > "This is my painting of apples. I learned apples have seeds and a core."

  > "This is how I can write my first and last name."

"These are the letters I know. These are the letters I need to work on."

Portfolios give teachers a way to show parents that their child is gaining skills or that previously discussed problematic behaviors are being addressed and redirected. Portfolios should display evidence of the child's nature and his growing awareness of it. Two sample portfolio pages can be found in appendix B. As you view them, notice the child's progress.

Portfolio Possibilities for Demonstration or Documentation of Skills

Demonstration and documentation of skills can be exhibited in many forms in portfolios. Below are assessment methods for portfolios, all of which are nurturing for a child with a must-move-to-learn nature. I tossed in a few quick insights and examples, such as cartoons (picture sequences), collages, and drawings.

- Experimenting: Use pictures of children performing science experiments as a form of assessment. Ask follow-up questions about the experiment, such as "What are you doing in this picture? You are holding a beaker. What did you use it for?"
- Interviewing: Interview students on discussed topics as a means of assessment; see Questioning below.
- Learning center pictures: See page 107 for various ideas.
    —Through impromptu and imaginative activities offered at learning centers, an extra busy nature can be observed, understood, and more readily explained.
- Map drawing: Have students draw and present a variety of maps, such as a map of the classroom, a map to the cafeteria, or a map of the school.
- Murals: Have students create a huge mural regarding a concept and present it to you as a form of assessment. Take a picture of it for the child's portfolio.
    —Painting can be a window to a child's thoughts and feelings. Watch samples closely during portfolio collection. Let small children use easels for variety when painting.

- Oral reading: Document fluency as a means of assessment.
- Paintings
- Questioning: Questioning extra busy children regarding what they have learned is an excellent way to use portfolios to nurture their nature. Make questions as open-ended and engaging as possible. I have found the following prompts helpful when questioning or interviewing for portfolios:

    Who said or did . . . ?

    Who might have done . . . ?

    Who seemed most likely to . . . ?

    Which one would best . . . ?

    Which blocks would . . . ?

    Which were most obvious?

    How did you do that?

    How might you have done that differently?

    Please describe . . .

    Please explain . . .

    Please list . . .

    Please name . . .

- Scrapbook pages: Assess a child's concept growth in areas such as the seasons, months of the year, or events in history.
- Stories: Assess a child's comprehension skills by having him retell or tell a story to you.
  —Reading and writing skills usually develop hand in hand. Oral reading is useful in developing both skills.
- Translating patterns: Assess math skills with this great hands-on method.
- Writing: Use letters and journal entries as a form of assessment.
  —Drawing can help extra busy children organize their thoughts before a writing activity.
  —Give each student a writing prompt that is of special interest to her. I've discovered that students write better with them.

In Closing . . .

Before leaping into chapter 4, remember that kinesthetic children have special and various methods of expression that are most obvious in their busy work patterns. Kinesthetic children are extraordinary investigators, and what you may view as off-task at times may actually be self-discovery and reflection. When redirecting kinesthetic learners, be flexible, hands-on, and supportive. Take time to closely observe the children at work. Openly and honestly evaluate what you see. You will never walk away without something new to question, expand upon, or nurture. Working with extra busy children is its own reward, generating a sense of wonder and fulfillment.

For further recommendations on effectively working with kinesthetic children at all developmental age levels, check out these resources:

Daily Preschool Experiences: For Learners at Every Level by Kay
    Hastings, Cathy Clemons, and April Montgomery (2008)
Take Time to See through Children's Eyes, CD (2007)
*Creating Inclusive Learning Environments for Young Children: What to
    Do on Monday Morning* by Clarissa Willis (2009)

All three resources are terrific additions to your Busy Bag. Suggest them to your students' parents as well.

Play is the work of children.

—ANNA FREUD

4

Ready, Set, Play

As a teacher of extra busy children, you know awake time is playtime. Children, especially extra busy children, require playtime. The importance of play for these kinesthetic-natured fireballs is equal to the importance of the air they breathe. *Play* plays a powerful part in helping extra busy children live happy, healthy, and productive lives. Extra busy children demand lots of time to play, as well as appropriate and safe spaces in which to carry it out. An extra busy child's play should be sensory-integrated and routinely physical, musical, and wet. Plenty of time for outdoor play adventures is important too.

For extra busy children, play is not an option but a must for their continually moving thoughts and bodies. Play is how an extra busy child discovers her world, expresses herself, and adapts to situations around her. Play is pertinent for an extra busy child's physical, intellectual, social, and emotional development at all age levels. It is especially healing and therapeutic for an extra busy child who is taunted at school or scolded a lot at home because of her extra busy tendencies. Play is an extra busy child's natural way to work out feelings and concerns and to deal with fears and insecurities. It is an avenue for developing and pursuing passions for a lifetime.

Play takes on many forms, and extra busy children benefit from a diverse menu. In this chapter, I discuss several forms of play, how each serves an essential purpose to the development and nature of the extra busy child, and how to get the most out of them.

> Play is the answer to the question, how does anything new ever come about?
> —Jean Piaget

Ahh. The power of play.

Constructive Play

Have you ever watched a child use blocks to build a tower? This is a simple form of constructive play. Constructive play can be defined as the manipulation of materials to construct things. It influences the growth and development of extra busy children. Constructive play

- encourages children to develop skills and peer relationships;
- inspires children to learn more about themselves and the world around them;
- enables children to rock their boat, to push their abilities;
- encourages creativity; and
- makes learning enjoyable.

Regular time for constructive and meaningful play can alleviate and redirect extra busy tendencies. The things an extra busy child can construct are limitless if time, support, and an array of materials are available.

Constructive Play Stuff

A few years ago I taught a workshop for early childhood educators that focused on constructive play. After considerable discussion with the primary teachers, it appeared that a majority of their young students preferred constructive play equipment referred to as "Stuff" over any available high-tech toy. At first, Stuff may appear to be mere junk to the adult eye, but to an extra busy child with an active imagination, the possibilities for use are endless.

As you look over the following chart of Stuff, keep in mind that the materials enrich all other forms of play discussed hereafter. Please watch children closely at all times when they are playing with the suggested materials. Older children can use items on lists for younger children.

Two to Three Years of Age

balls (various large sizes)

bandanas

baskets (all shapes, sizes, and textures)

blocks (large, wooden and plastic)

bowls (plastic, all sizes)

bows (various colors)

boxes (all sizes)

cereal boxes

chalk (oversized for outdoor use)

clay

clothes (old and oversized)

crates (plastic)

cups (paper and plastic)

dolls (all ethnic groups)

egg cartons

eye patches

funnels

gloves

hats

kitchen utensils (old, large)

milk cartons or jugs

newspaper for crumpling

oatmeal boxes

pails

paper bags

paper plates (all sizes)

plastic containers (all sizes)

playdough

pots and pans (all sizes)

sand

shoe boxes

shovels

sponges (colored and larger sizes)

tubs (plastic)

wagons for transporting dirt, sand, or Stuff

Four to Five Years of Age

beads

bottles of bubbles

clothespins

cotton swabs

craft feathers

envelopes

index cards

leaves (dry or fresh)

magazines

mirrors (nonbreakable handheld or full size)

muffin tin liners

outdated calendars

paintbrushes (all sizes)

paper (colored construction, cardstock, computer, crepe—the options are endless)

pie tins

pillowcases

pine cones

pipe cleaners/chenille stems

playdough

play money

postcards

ribbons

shoelaces

sponges (colored and all sizes)

spoons

straws (bendable)

string

toy people, animals, and vehicles

whistles

wooden craft sticks

yarn

Six to Seven Years of Age

acorns

aluminum foil

bottle caps

bouncy balls and jacks

bulk items from bargain bins after holidays (for example, face paint and fake fingernails after Halloween; doilies and cards after Valentine's Day; small nutcracker soldiers and plastic ornaments after Christmas)

buttons

candles for mud pies, clay cakes, or sand castle decor

cans

coat hangers (plastic)

coffee cans

counters (any group of small objects that can be counted, sorted, or manipulated for classroom learning purposes, such as buttons, tiles, marbles, felt cutouts, nuts, seeds, dried beans, pasta, seashells)

doll furniture (miniature)

film canisters

flower pots

paper umbrellas (sold to put in beverages; clip the sharp ends)

ping-pong balls

rubber bands

seeds

sequins

shells

spools (with or without thread)

toothpicks

treasures (polished stones, shells, jewels)

twist ties

wallpaper scraps

Encouraging Constructive Play with Stuff

Busy Bag Trick
To get the best play possibilities from Stuff, make it portable. A great transporting idea for constructive play Stuff is turning an old tackle box into a tote box.

I have observed that the following things happen when extra busy children engage in constructive play:

- They become engrossed in (and therefore focused on) what they are trying to accomplish through their play.
- Their personalities come to life.
- They are not easily distracted from their play.
- They suddenly become fearless—confident in their abilities—and the challenges they encounter are taken in stride.
- Time restraints vanish.
- Prior problems disappear.

The following suggestions will help you encourage constructive play:

- **Realize that extra busy children need to engage in constructive play.**
  Constructive play is an essential building block for children—a critical part of the foundation they need in order to develop properly. Constructive play is as relevant as nutritious food.
- **Constructive play doesn't have to cost anything—really.**
  Some of the best constructive play toys are outside, in nature, not from a store. Every home has constructive play Stuff. Toddlers love pots and pans from the kitchen; older children love to play dress-up with old costumes or clothing.
- **Don't force constructive play, or any other play for that matter.**
  When Bella was three, I enrolled her in ballet classes. She wasn't thrilled, and her participation conveyed her attitude toward the forced activity. Be aware of what an extra busy child likes and dislikes. Not all children like to dig deep in icky, sticky stuff or make mud pies. Be sensitive to individual needs. Play is the work of children, but it shouldn't be stressful, competitive, or joyless.

- **Play dates are effective for constructive play.**
  Children learn to socialize and develop relationships as they play together. Empathy, compassion, and sharing are a few of the developmental milestones children pass as they play with one another. Bella plays best in groups of three—any more than that and she becomes overwhelmed. Every child is different.

- **Bark (loudly) about recess time for constructive play time.**
  As I write, I am looking forward to a long, vigorous swim. It is my time to unwind and relax. Children are no different. If your school or preschool center is shortening recess, be an advocate and share the importance of it with administrators. Outside play time for hands-on constructive play is vanishing in schools across the county. We need to protect our children's rights and access to constructive play.

Constructive Play Centers

Constructive play can be very simple and made readily available through what educators call "learning centers." "Learning centers are places set up in the classroom where students can engage in hands-on activities that allow them to obtain additional experience in using new skills, expand on skill usage to more closely match their individual needs, and work cooperatively with other students" (Herrell and Jordan 2004, 110). Clear behavior expectations and sensory-integrated procedures should be associated with each constructive play center. Effective constructive play centers focus on

- learning by doing—encouraging discovery, exploration, and wonderment;
- providing multiple techniques and methods of learning;
- individualizing play;
- providing positive reinforcement;
- developing accountability for learning;
- sharing, talking, and socializing;

- allowing children to choose an activity that addresses their personal goals and meets their needs; and
- offering regularly changing creative Stuff.

Constructive Play Center Ideas

Listed below are classroom learning center possibilities, as well as a few fabulous others useful for extra busy kinesthetic learners. Constructive play can be made available through independent home learning centers. Share the following learning center ideas with your busy bees' parents.

Art Center: Gather textured stamps and stencils, colored construction paper, and an assortment of markers, crayons, and colored pencils. Offer a variety of writing supplies (fat and skinny, bold and pastel colors). Make playdough, modeling clay, and goopy, gooey materials (see chapter 5) readily available in plastic containers.

Busy Bag Trick
Shortening and a few drops of food coloring make a fabulous face paint. Avoid the eye area.

Dramatic Play Center: Raid thrift stores for old clothing and theme costumes (such as firefighter, doctor, nurse, farmer, or airline pilot). Toss everything into a designated box. Get extra creative and toss in a roll of toilet paper for mummy play. Add age-appropriate and safe accessories, such as costume jewelry, makeup, hats of all sorts and sizes, gloves, necklaces, goggles, belts, neckties, scarves, and, of course, a huge mirror for admiring the results. Don't forget literacy props such as menus, food ordering forms, or pretend prescription and phone message pads.

Listening Center: Use books on tape and CDs to hone listening and comprehension skills. Set up a listening center with an old tape or CD player for a child to use independently. Local libraries offer books on tape and CDs to check out.

Cooking Center: In my primary classroom I used cooking centers as incentives for my students. They enjoyed making instant pudding and other snacks with visual cue cards. Many kinesthetic skills can be nurtured through a cooking center, including cutting, shaping, kneading, mixing, spreading, measuring, and scooping.

Snacking Center: A snacking center can teach healthy food choices, hand washing, and social skills to use while snacking. Incorporate a variety of the textured snack foods suggested in chapter 6.

Manipulative Center: Use counters (see page 104) for sorting activities (color, shape, and size) or for counting by ones, fives, and tens.

Science Center: Constructive learning center possibilities that focus on science are endless. A series of skill-building activities can be offered with the use of balance scales, rulers, graded cups for liquids, prisms, magnets, magnifying materials, stethoscopes, microscopes, kaleidoscopes, and plants. Add graph paper, data sheets, a measuring tape, and blueprint paper.

Gadget Center: Unscrewing and taking apart old appliances, like toasters, is fascinating to children. Broken clocks and cameras, and nuts, bolts, washers, and screws can catapult extra busy creative thoughts. Garage sales are hot spots for equipping a gadget center. As always, consider age appropriateness with a gadget center.

Alphabet Center: Set up flannelboards and felt letters for letter identification and matching games. Or let children sing along and record an alphabet song, then press rewind and listen to the new song.

Animal Hospital Center: Use stuffed animals as patients. Toy doctor sets are reasonably priced at discount stores.

Pet Center: Acquire a small classroom pet that children can watch and take turns feeding. Examples from my primary classrooms include newts, water turtles, fish, gerbils, guinea pigs, and rabbits. A well-caged tarantula is also

Extra busy children often enjoy counting coins made of diced carrots or patterning a rainbow vegetable kabob on skewers (with supervision). Use a variety of colored veggies such as red, yellow, and green peppers; cauliflower; cucumbers; red onions; broccoli; and eggplant.

an option (the tarantula molting process fascinated my students). Raise a butterfly. You can rely on a caterpillar discovered by an extra busy child rather than a store bought or commercial project. Set up an aquarium, terrarium, or indoor ant farm.

Outdoor Observation Center: Section off an ant colony for viewing purposes. Let children watch it grow after establishing safety guidelines. Put up bird feeders with seeds and sugar water for a bird watching center. Let children draw the birds they observe.

Laundry Center: Obtain an old washboard, some soap, and a few articles of clothing. String a low clothes line and provide clothespins as an extension idea. See chapter 4 for other excellent water play possibilities.

Hula Ball Center: Hang a Hula-hoop from a tree branch so children can toss balls of different sizes and textures back and forth through the hoop. Children can count their catches and misses.

Be original with your ideas. Lock into the extra busy child's formula for ticking to inspire mighty constructive play. Here are some additional learning center possibilities:

- block center
- computer center
- library center
- music center
- pouring center
- woodworking center
- kitchen center
- store center
- restaurant center
- hair salon center

And remember, constructive play centers can be moved outdoors in appropriate weather.

Busy Bag Trick
Picnic tables make great additions for accommodating outside constructive play centers. For example, move a listening center outdoors onto one. Set up an outdoor stage for a dramatic play area on another.

Mount a huge mailbox for regularly used outdoor learning center Stuff. Old suitcases, laundry baskets, or bags are doable—even an old lunch box will work.

You've been there many times: While working with a small group of children, you observe Juan's extra busy energy begin bubbling. Soon he's ready to explode. But in which direction?

Extra busy children never have enough room to roam. Standing in a cafeteria line, waiting to go outside, sitting quietly while waiting for the teacher—these are all torturous to extra busy children. They want to move, but they're limited to a small space. The secret to tackling these limited-space issues is advocating for sufficient space and adjusting to the child's busy nature. Easier said than done, right?

Developing limited-space thinking with extra busy children isn't as difficult as one might think. A little creativity and some trial and error are sure to get the ball rolling. Besides, we were all children once. Think back to your childhood days of imaginative play: ant watching with a magnifying glass; fort building with pillows, blankets, and kitchen table chairs; bike riding until dusk; and tree climbing on hot summer days. Now think about carrying a diaper bag for your own or for other children. (It still amazes me how much stuff little people need for a single thirty-minute outing!) Combine these two trains of thought to discover the first principle of managing limited-space play with extra busy children.

Have you noticed how children love gadgets, gizmos, and those annoying prize machines at store exits? The toy inside the plastic bubble is worthless, but children are thrilled with the element of wonder: "What is it? What does it do?" Extra busy children take this to the nth degree. They have built-in radar for actively investigating everything and everyone around them—usually in an intense manner. Knowing this, take advantage of it when confined. Stock up on limited-space equipment, including self-stick notes, note pads, buttons, crayons, strings, yarn, rubber bands, and noodles for a Keep 'Em Busy bag. Discount or dollar stores are great for supplies. Keep in mind, the more strange or novel the Keep 'Em Busy bag contents, the more imaginative the play.

Strengthening the Home-School Connection

Parents encounter limited spaces all the time— waiting in line at a grocery store, sitting in a doctor's office, sick days, and long "Are we there yet?" car rides. Share Keep 'Em Busy bag ideas with your parents. They'll be sure to thank you.

Keep 'Em Busy Bag Ideas

Busy Bag Trick
To alleviate project messes, I suggest keeping individual projects in small brown paper bags. The bag can act as a mat for play, and it makes for easy and quick cleanup. Keep a few wet wipes in a sealed bag for a fast wipe down as well.

Please consider age appropriateness and supervision needs for all activities. Keep the activities as sensory-integrated as possible.

Bag of Dough: Put several small balls of differently colored playdough in a small brown paper bag. Let the extra busy child play with the dough balls, using the bag as a mat. Include a marker for doodling on the bag afterward. Easy playdough recipes can be found in chapter 5.

Colored Clips: Put a handful or two of colored paper clips in a resealable container. With a child, link a patterned train together while waiting.

Spelling Words: Practice spelling words while waiting. Have a child write spelling words on craft sticks. Younger children can practice writing their names. Use narrower wooden craft sticks to hone focusing and fine motor skills.

Beads: Include a small butter container filled with colorful beads and string. Let the child string a patterned bracelet or necklace while waiting.

Stickers: Draw circles on a piece of paper. Let the child practice one-to-one correspondence by placing one sticker inside each circle. Draw circles the same size or smaller than the stickers. This activity also builds fine motor skills. Visit www.medibadge.com or www.smilemakers.com for fabulous sticker deals and ideas.

Webs: Give a child a handful of white webbing (from a craft store or discounted Halloween sale) or strips of transparent tape. Ask her to make shapes. Both are excellent fine motor activities, and children enjoy fiddling with the materials.

Egg Cartons: Put half an egg carton (cardboard works best), tape, string, crayons, and a small pair of round-ended scissors in a brown paper bag. Watch what the extra busy child does with the supplies.

Pipe Cleaners: Include various colored pipe cleaners/chenille stems for braiding or bending into objects.

Toy Catalog: Pack along an old toy catalog for a child to look through, cut pictures out of, or circle wish list items in.

Finger Faces: Draw faces on your fingers and the child's with washable markers. Tell puppet stories.

Decorated Bookmarks: Make bookmarks out of precut colored cardstock. Have the child decorate them.

Books on Tape: Give the child an old personal cassette tape player and an accompanying storybook and tape.

ABCs: Choose a letter from the alphabet. On a note pad, draw the letter. Have the child turn it into a picture. For example, make a rabbit out of R, an octopus out of O, or a lizard out of L. Bump the activity up a level by adding adjectives. "Draw an odd-looking octopus. Draw a red rabbit."

Matching Play: File folder games are quick and versatile. Laminate folders with matching games. Use Velcro adhesive tape for the pieces. On the right is a picture of a season sorting folder game I made for Bella.

Hole Punching: Give the child a hole punch and some cardstock. Draw squiggly lines or write his name on the sturdy paper so he can punch along it.

Hobbies: Start a collection or hobby for limited space play. The key to a worthwhile collection is engaging the child's independent imagination, locking into her interests and formula for ticking. Ask yourself, "What amuses this busy bee?" Great starting ideas include memory books, scrap albums, and sewing, beading, or trading cards. Collecting buttons, bottle caps, coins, stamps, flowers, leaves, or napkins from various places can be fun too. Get an extra

busy child a special backpack for toting the collection to and from limited space play areas.

Patterns: Have three differently colored self-stick note pads for the extra busy child to stack in AB and ABC patterns. Add to the action by drawing a cartoon to flip through.

Paper: Give the child a sheet of notebook paper and ask him to tear an object out of it, such as an apple, a banana, or a star.

Saltine Shapes: Saltine crackers are great for being nibbled into shapes by extra busy children.

Sculptures: Turn colored construction paper and rubber bands into creations. Roll, bend, twist, or tie them. Spare bank deposit slips work well too.

Share these ideas with parents:

- Sprawling out in a corner of a waiting room can prove relaxing. Once in your corner, have a staring contest with the child.
- Stash a sturdy paper tube in your Keep 'Em Busy bag, and take turns listening to each other's heartbeat.
- Schedule doctor's appointments first thing in the morning. Chances are you'll get in and out faster.
- If you find an extra busy child on the verge of throwing a fit, take him outside for a five-minute break. Have the child do a few pop-ups to settle down. Tell the child "Crouch down and wrap your arms around your knees. When I tap you on the head, jump as high as you can."
- Throw a couple of pieces of sidewalk chalk or a small plastic magnifying glass in a Keep 'Em Busy bag for outside breaks.
- Use baby wipe containers to hold trading cards, crayons, or markers. Turn one into a first-aid kit for your Keep 'Em Busy bag.
- Insect bites can be particularly bothersome to an extra busy child, especially in limited spaces. Pack calamine lotion in an old, clean film canister and let the child use a paintbrush to decorate the bug bites. Pump up the activity by having the child count the number of bites out loud.

Cell Phone: Hand a child an old cell phone so she can practice dialing her home telephone number. Have her recite it back to you. Rehearsing the number out loud to a familiar tune can make it easier to memorize.

Chopsticks: For a sensory-integrated Keep 'Em Busy bag snack, pack a small plastic container of cooked brown rice. With the child, practice using chopsticks. This will not only make a wait yummy but also hone focusing and fine motor skills. Sorting colored fish or oyster crackers can make a wait tasty too.

Sticker Tag: Play sticker tag with a child. Each of you will need five stickers. Let the child first stick one on your face. You put one in the same spot on him. Play until all your stickers are stuck.

Toothpick Caterpillars: Put a few toothpicks and colored gum drops in a sandwich bag to make patterned caterpillars together. Break toothpicks in half for legs.

Use limited-space time to enjoy, accept, and nurture extra busy children. Ultimately, this time is what you make of it. If you want to sit on the floor with an extra busy child to play a game of Go Fish or Hangman, do so. Find an available corner, if possible. In her book *101 Activities for Kids in Tight Spaces* (1995), Carol Stock Kranowitz recommends that readers get their minds around sensory integration in restricted quarters by thinking of a five-year-old child participating in Ring Around the Rosy. The game allows the child to experience continual touching, bumping, looking, listening, giggling, getting up quickly, running, and falling down, while loving every sensory-integrated minute of it. Extra busy children stay engaged longer with sensory-integrated exercises. Simon Says and the Itsy Bitsy Spider are great sensory-integrated movement activities to try in limited space.

Read

Any time is a terrific time to read to an extra busy child, but a wait at the doctor's office, or a day sick in bed, is especially a good use of time for reading. A great read-aloud book is sure to make others waiting in the office chuckle. Be interactive with the story; use voice variation for characters. Consider the child's attention span when making your selections. Here are two wonderful books:

Dogs Don't Wear Sneakers by Laura Numeroff is a great rhyming book with wonderful personified animal illustrations.

Peanut Butter Rhino by Vincent Andriani is a silly and simply illustrated book. Rhino loses one of his two peanut butter sandwiches and must find it before a scheduled lunch date with Elephant. While looking and asking friends, he doesn't realize his sandwich is stuck to his bottom.

Create Oxymorons

Oxymorons—concepts made of contradictory words—are hilarious and smile producing. Here are a few of my favorites: "alone together," "jumbo shrimp," and "same difference." Get creative with your choices. Knock-knock joke possibilities are endless, and although Bella's are senseless, like those of most young children, I enjoy her imagination and silliness.

Things to Remember during Limited-Space Play

- **Extra busy children respond best to calm choices.**
  "Will you please sit still?" isn't the wisest thing to say to extra busy children. Try positive reinforcement with multiple choices instead, such as

  "Sammy, I know you are frustrated because we have to wait our turn to go to music class. Pull out the colored noodle bag and string me a pattern or count all the coins in my change purse."

  "Emma, I know it is hard to wait for the speech therapist. Would you like to play a game of oxymorons or tell knock-knock jokes? You can go first."

- **Always consider what's best for an extra busy child during time in limited spaces.**

If an extra busy child is tired, hungry, or just crabby, having him wait to work with you probably isn't the best idea. I always ask myself, Is this the hill I want to collapse on with Bella?

- **Accept that limited-space projects can be messy.**
  Extra busy children learn from creativity. Whether it comes from a baggie full of homemade playdough to occupy time or glitter and glue at the table on a dreary day, accepting that creativity can and will make a mess spares many headaches.

- **Rushing extra busy children only makes matters worse.**
  As an adult, do you like being rushed? Do you start something five minutes before you know you'll have to quit? Then why impose such a predicament on an extra busy child? Plan the contents of your Keep 'Em Busy bag according to the amount of limited-space time. If the waiting is over but the extra busy child isn't finished with her game or project, work with other students until her task is complete. It'll beat the outburst from an interrupted train of busy thoughts.

Finally, keep in mind that wherever you go with an extra busy child, there you are. *Any place* becomes what you make of it.

Outdoor Play

The natural world is a vast playground just waiting to be explored. As a child, if the weekend sun was shining, my siblings and I were out building forts and playing endless games of Tag or Hide-and-Seek. Unfortunately, children today spend less time enjoying nature's gifts than ever before. One would assume that jumping into a pile of fall leaves or splashing in puddles of sweet-smelling rain would motivate children to be outdoors, but technology appears to be more of a draw. Days of carefree outside play for children appear to be long gone.

I highly recommend the book *Last Child in the Woods: Saving Our Children from Nature-Deficit Disorder* by Richard Louv (2005) for your Busy Bag. This revolutionary book boldly depicts the necessity of nature in children's lives and shows how time in nature can tremendously help children, especially extra busy children, in the areas of obesity, attention problems, depression, stress, emotional growth, and even academics.

Paul Dayton, winner of an E. O. Wilson Naturalist Award, recommends Louv's book, writing, "Every parent should read [Louv's] book, but equally important, every teacher should take it to heart and take every student into nature." Louv points out the following from a study published by the Children's Hospital and Regional Medical Center in Seattle: "Each hour of TV watched per day by preschoolers increases by 10 percent the likelihood that they will develop concentration problems and other symptoms of attention-deficit disorders by age seven" (Louv 2005, 102). "Studies suggest that nature may be useful as a therapy for Attention Deficit Hyperactivity Disorder (ADHD), used with or, when appropriate, even replacing medications or behavioral therapies" (100).

It is more important than ever that you initiate positive steps toward getting extra busy children outdoors for essential time in the natural world.

The Play Garden

Although natural outdoor play areas that children can investigate and frolic in are slowly disappearing with every passing year, you can propel extra busy children to their best playground—the natural world is literally waiting outside their door.

Every year in the spring I plant a garden with Bella. It usually consists of towering corn stalks to dodge in and out of and small pumpkins to carve in the fall. A few summers ago, in addition to the garden, my husband and I put in a pond filled with inexpensive fish and tadpoles. We planted colorful flowers to attract ladybugs and butterflies. Bella found the play garden to be a magical place. We marveled as she and neighborhood friends generated natural play games—"Who can catch the tadpoles the fastest?" and "Who can catch the most fish in a bucket?"

As an educator and parent, I've designed a few play gardens over the years. There are a few things to know before you start construction on a play garden for an extra busy child:

- Homemade play gardens are adventure areas where children

can reclaim the magic of original childhood play with natural materials, such as sticks, branches, old logs, stones, mud, sand, trees, dirt, leaves, grass, flowers, and water, and spaces, such as climbing and hiding areas.

- The idea behind a play garden is to use the landscape and vegetation as the play setting and nature as the play element.

- Play gardens should advocate quiet time, creativity, and, of course, the outdoors. The play garden should serve as a child's place only. No adults allowed.

Extra busy children will soon see a play garden as a special place to get away—a place that activates a world described in fairy tales and myths. Building a play garden isn't as difficult or expensive as it may sound. The task requires some planning and imagining, and, most important, locking into an extra busy child's formula for ticking. Listed below are easy and purposeful ways to develop a simple play garden for an extra busy child. Review the Stuff listed earlier in this chapter to use for accenting gardens for constructive outdoor play.

Sandboxes: Do you remember plunging your hands and feet in warm, wet sand as a child? I sure do! My siblings and I would take turns burying each other deep in it. Sandboxes or sandpits with easy in-and-out access are fabulous for an outdoor sensory play garden. Oversized tires filled with sand are great for seated sandbox play. Pump up the play experience with water for building sand castles or making special sand cakes. Fill the sandbox with sturdy plastic cups, bowls, old strainers, funnels, spoons, or any other Stuff. Here are a few super sand play ideas:

- Use cookie cutters to draw in cool, wet sand.
- Bury toys and have the child try to find them.
- Scatter seashells and pebbles in the sand for a make-believe beach adventure.
- Create roads and moats for toy cars, boats, and trucks.
- Place a small scale on a sturdy box for scientific weighing purposes.

Busy Bag Trick

Covering the sand-box after each use is important, especially if cats prowl the neighborhood. Don't allow food in sandboxes; bees and other bugs can be attracted to spills. Store sand toys in a covered bin after each use.

Busy Bag Trick

A speedy way to remove sand from extra busy children is to sprinkle baby powder on the child's sandy skin and then brush it off.

- Sprinkle fine, colored sand about for variety.
- Teach a child how to draw and play tic-tac-toe with a stick in the sand.
- Hide ice cubes in cool sand in the evening. Let the child walk through with her eyes closed to discover chilling sensations.

Water: Water is a sensory medium extra busy children naturally enjoy. Small ponds, dug-out moats, trenches, and waterfalls are great for supervised water play. Wading pools and water tables filled with buckets, turn wheels, and spray bottles are suitable play garden ideas. Additional outdoor water play ideas can be found later in this chapter.

Mud Areas: The joy and sensory stimulation of making mud pies with toy shovels and buckets is excellent hands-on play. Many extra busy children delight in squishing their toes into mud too. Make animal and castle mud sculptures. Use Stuff for small details like eyes and drawbridges. Turn a mud area into an outside kitchen center for whipping up more than pies. Big sturdy boxes can be turned into a sink and stove. Gather old cooking utensils, pots, pans, and containers for cooking mud soup. Mix mud with pebbles, dry leaves, bark chunks, grass blades, hay strands, and a few shakes of sand as salt. Let the child see you get creative.

Stepping Stones: Textured stepping stones make outstanding sensory play for extra busy children. Place a sensory path in an outdoor play garden. Hobby stores offer flat stones that can easily be turned into different pathways for extra busy children to skip and hop along. Or situate and purposely texture sturdy metal pie pans or old Frisbees for a shoeless sensory pathway—bumpy, rough, prickly, gritty, smooth. Textured balance beams, tunnels, or age-appropriate ramps are possibilities for enhancing stepping-stone pathways. Tires or Hula-hoops are also options for creating a stepping path.

Dirt-Digging Areas: Extra busy children will discover and explore textures as they pack mud, sift sand, and dig dirt. Hole

Busy Bag Trick
Great Gardens for Kids by Clare Matthews is loaded with ideas and detailed photographs of stimulating fantasy play gardens. Also, *365 Outdoor Activities You Can Do with Your Child* by Steven J. Bennett and Ruth Bennett is a must read for ideas that will stimulate imaginative outside play that entertains, educates, and delights.

digging greatly appeals to extra busy children. I'm convinced the repetitive movement of the task—scoop, dump, scoop, dump—soothes them. Filling deep holes with water for homemade boating adventures is even more intriguing to busy bees. Extra busy boys and girls enjoy using chunky trucks with scoops for dirt play. If possible, create small dirt hills for extra busy children to climb on and dig in. Bury plastic worms and bugs, twigs, acorns, small stones, lemon and orange peels, pinecones, and other little treasures for a sensory explosion.

Grass and Flowers: A small bench on a patch of grass surrounded by a few pretty flowers can be a very special place for an extra busy little person. Running, crawling, or playing in lush green grass with wild flowers can be a captivating experience for small extra busy children. Here are some specific outdoor flower and grass ideas:

• Together with a child, choose and plant flowers in each color of the rainbow for a lovely, educational rainbow flower garden. Start with simple flowers such as marigolds

and zinnias. When Farrah was small, I planted sunflowers
for her; she marveled at their height.

- Give an extra busy child a magnifying glass to snoop
  around with while down on his knees in the grass.
- Spread out a big, comfy blanket on grass. Lie down with
  the child, commenting together on the shapes of clouds or
  groups of stars.
- Shade an area with a tarp or canvas. Situate stumps and
  logs to sit on in a play garden, observing nature or reading
  books. Make binoculars and periscopes available.

Tree Houses and Forts: Although outdoor tree houses can be
elaborate, they can also be very simple. Several refrigerator,
washer, or dryer boxes work wonders for a quick play
garden fort.

Homemade Tire Swings, Rope Ladders, and Climbing Nets:
Extra busy children can benefit tremendously from swinging
and climbing. Come to think of it, I've never seen a child

swinging or climbing and frowning at the same time. Swinging directly targets a child's tactile sense—wind whooshing, legs thrusting, arms pumping. Tire swinging is excellent physical play too.

Hay: If the child is not allergic to them, hay bales are fantastic for sitting on or leaning against. They can be used for shelter, shade, or different climbing levels in a play garden. Hay bales can also be situated to offer children nooks and crannies for enjoying privacy or to make mazes for crawling through.

Wind Chimes, Wind Socks, and Outdoor Streamers: Promoting purposeful outdoor experiences starts with allowing young children to connect with and participate in nature. Wind chimes and wind socks are wonderful ways to achieve this goal. Wind chimes, wind socks, and outdoor streamers bring nature to life for children visually and aurally. Hang wind chimes or outdoor streamers from trees or fences. Let the child make one to hang in her play garden.

Small Vegetable Gardens: If you don't have room for a garden, use a window box or a few small pots. Growing gardens is a great way to incorporate nature into an extra busy child's life as well as to work on critical thinking skills. The characteristics of plants can be observed and taught first hand. For example, pumpkins are vine plants that grow horizontally, while corn stalks grow vertically. The basics of living things can be introduced to extra busy children: living things need water and sunlight to grow. Even at the young age of four, Bella did a wonderful job of watering her plants every day. A few of her plants perished. She quickly discovered how plants choke to death if overtaken by weeds. Bella even noticed the effects of New Mexico's hot, dry weather on her pumpkin garden.

Logs: Nature is at its best under a log. Place one in a play garden and then roll it over a week or two later so children can observe what's going on underneath. Talk about

Busy Bag Trick

Peas and radishes are fabulous first-time vegetable garden plants. They grow super fast. Carrots are amazing for extra busy children to harvest. Most children know carrots only from bags.

what they see. A quick reminder: children should observe carefully, but not touch.

As you plan a play garden, keep your ultimate goal in mind—to get the extra busy child to recognize the natural beauty and learning environment of the outdoors. Work from the extra busy child's interests and formula for ticking. Subtly provoke, model, and suggest ideas. You might use personal stories and experiences: "When I was little I built forts outside. I still remember exactly what I used. Would you like to make one together?" Ultimately though, let the child decide what he wants to make of his outdoor play adventures.

Finally, I'd like to share a picture with you; it's a pumpkin patch play garden we planted a few years back. I found a small bench at a garage sale for Bella to sit on near the pumpkin patch. The bench isn't in view, but you can see the old wooden gate leaning against the wall and the small pond with inexpensive annuals. The garden invites play, a key objective of outdoor play experiences.

Physical play, often called "gross motor play," involves large-muscle body movement. Extra busy children need to engage daily in some form of physical play for energy release. Experts recommend that children engage in at least sixty minutes of physical activity daily. Try not to confuse gross motor play with fine motor play. Examples of gross motor play include galloping, running, skipping, hopping, walking, leaping, jumping, tossing, throwing, catching, dancing, stretching, and balancing. Fine motor play involves the small muscles of the hands and fingers working in coordination with the eyes. Examples of fine motor play activities that improve hand-eye coordination include using scissors or a pencil, gluing, coloring, or steadily beading a necklace. Stapling, drawing, hammering, tracing, and weaving are options as well.

Both forms of movement tremendously benefit an extra busy child's ability to focus. The next few pages will focus on *gross* physical play for releasing extra busy energy.

Benefits of Physical Play

Regular physical play helps extra busy children in many ways:

- Physical play naturally relaxes extra busy children. It soothes them and releases bottled up extra energy. Don't you feel great after a good workout?

- Physical play helps extra busy children focus and stay alert. Busy children often fidget intensely because of a nature that screams for movement. When excess anxiety or frustration is released through physical play, the attention span increases. This is highly beneficial for sustained academic learning. Regular strenuous physical play helps extra busy children control their impulses, which is advantageous in a classroom setting.

- Physical play helps extra busy children maintain proper body weight. It isn't a secret that many young children today are overweight. Regular physical play helps extra busy children

Strengthening the Home-School Connection

Encourage parents to squeeze in physical play with a child while doing errands by marching up stairs or parking at the end of the parking lot and walking zig-zag to your destination. If possible, walk a child to and from school, using the time to talk.

keep their weight in check; it improves their overall health as well.

- Physical play helps extra busy children sleep better. Children will naturally sleep better when tuckered out. The body adjusts, and craves a good night's sleep after a day of hard physical play.

As you ponder productive physical play possibilities, keep the following in mind:

- Extra busy children will be more eager to engage in physical play if the play and skills involved are age appropriate. Expecting a child to participate and be successful in a physical game requiring skills she isn't able to perform will backfire.
- Extra busy children will more readily engage in physical play—both indoors and outdoors—if their environment encourages it.
- Extra busy children will look forward to physical play if a variety of experiences are regularly made available. Participate in physical play activities with the children. Suggestions are listed below.

Increasing an Extra Busy Child's Physical Play Time

The following are ways to increase the amount and variety of physical play in an extra busy child's routine:

Just take the child outside. Hook a child up with a jump rope, Hula-hoop, Frisbee, yo-yo, or an aluminum can for a game of Kick the Can. Marbles, jacks, and sidewalk chalk are great too. The fresh air will be invigorating and encourage physical play.

Model regular physical play. We need to model physical play activities. Modeling simple physical games with children is a starting point for instilling healthy, active adult habits. Try the following physical play games and activities with the children:

- Hopscotch

Busy Bag Trick

All you need for a quick outside game of Hopscotch is a small rock and a piece of sidewalk chalk. (I always carry both in a Keep 'Em Busy bag.) If short on chalk, a stick for drawing a game in the dirt will do. Pump up the physical movement by having an extra busy child jump on one leg while clapping. Get creative.

Tell parents to turn off the TV. I'll be straight to the point regarding my opinion of the tube: it is robbing our children of valuable playing and learning experiences. The television, as well as video games, prevent children from

- playing
- being creative
- writing and reading
- developing the ability to concentrate for long periods of time
- socializing and developing relationships with others
- thinking critically
- imagining
- exercising
- being outdoors
- challenging abilities
- practicing gross and fine motor skills
- practicing hand-eye coordination (Stoppard 2001, 135)

Parents should limit their extra busy child's time with electronic media. This includes computer usage and Internet access, which should be monitored closely.

- Twister
- Musical Chairs
- Head, Shoulders, Knees, and Toes
- Freeze Tag, chasing, or races—"I'll race you to the fence and back!"
- Red Rover, Red Rover
- The Hokey Pokey
- Tug of War
- Red Light, Green Light
- Crab Walk or Wheelbarrow Walk
- Sock Skating on smooth floors (paper plates work too)
- Egg-and-Spoon Races
- Balloon Ball (It's easy: Bounce the balloon back and forth with the child, keeping it off the floor. Use paddles for variety.)
- Hot Potato
- Leapfrog
- Mother May I
- Duck, Duck, Goose
- HORSE (You'll need a basketball hoop for this one.)
- Dodgeball

Whether an extra busy child is naturally drawn to physical experiences or has to be nudged in the right direction, regular physical play will definitely trim down extra busy habits and possible extra pounds. Set aside time each day to get physically active with the extra busy child. Physical play can be an uplifting time for an extra busy child, who can expend extra energy while you burn off stress too. Just start moving. Just get physical. Just play.

Water Play (and Consumption)

Bella and I are biased toward water play. We both love the sensation of being fully immersed in water. Bella, like most young extra busy children I have worked with, is fascinated with water—and its play possibilities.

I discovered its fascinating power for myself in 2003. The year was tumultuous for our family, full of raw emotions and changes. We welcomed Bella into the family, my sister lost her battle with cancer, and I trudged through graduate school, craving a break but fearing I'd never return if I dropped out for a while. This roller coaster ride plunged my entire being into severe and unbearable anxiety. I was a knot of nerves, to say the least, and Bella's intense colic did not help matters. After what seemed like endless days of shaking hands and racing thoughts, I gave in and went to see my doctor. "I do not want a pill—no quick fix," I immediately and forcefully explained. "I am breast-feeding. What can I do to relieve my nerves and all the excess mental noise in my head naturally?"

"Well," my doctor began after a long pause, "the best alternative remedy I can offer is water. Start drinking lots of water, and take up lap swimming. Vigorous swimming is one of the most effective and natural ways to alleviate stress, anxiety, and depression. It'll help you focus, and sleep better too."

In my head I said, "What?" looking at him as if he hadn't heard a word I'd said. Departing, skeptical, I decided to give it a whirl. What did I have to lose?

The next morning I ventured to our health club and stood before its indoor pool. I eventually waded in. At first the water was sharp and not accepting, but that changed within minutes. Suddenly, my rigid body and jittery mind felt support and freedom. The splashing sound and movement of the natural medium relaxed me. Forty-five minutes of vigorous lap swimming later, I emerged, focused and extremely refreshed. I was instantly and therapeutically hooked. Not much has changed in my swimming routine since 2003, except that Bella joins me several times a week in the pool so she can expend some of her extra energy too. I swim forty to fifty laps daily to ward off stress, anxiety, and depression, all of which are hereditary problems.

Most people know that when it is consumed regularly, water is awesome for the body's systems. Playing in it and chugging adequate amounts daily can prove beneficial for extra busy children too. Bella's busyness is dramatically alleviated with regular supervised swimming sessions combined with water play.

Benefits of Water

Water consumption and water play are powerful tools for helping children, especially extra busy children, thrive. Water play allows for increased mobility, awareness of body movement, and relaxation. It also relieves tension and anxiety. Whether slurping a large glass or splashing around in a pool, an extra busy child will greatly benefit from water and its play possibilities. Listed below are specific benefits of water and its play:

- **Water is fantastic sensory play for extra busy children.**
  When it comes to play materials, most extra busy children don't mind getting wet or messy. This fact makes water play enjoyable, especially on hot days.
- **Water helps regulate body weight.**
  Encouraging extra busy children to drink water can be beneficial to their health and aid in regulating their weight. Modeling such behavior is ideal. Children also naturally enjoy the sensation of water, making supervised water play an excellent exercise for promoting weight maintenance.
- **Water is great for therapy.**
  Licensed therapists and teachers use a variety of water-play techniques. A major part of my graduate study included water play as therapy for several of my extra busy students with special needs. Regular water play greatly enhanced their overall performance and attitude in school.

Water play fosters a variety of skill development. Water is a great medium for addressing physical, cognitive, and psycho-social needs. Goals are selected based on a thorough evaluation of the child and his needs. Treatment activities may be selected to help address physical needs such as range of motion, flexibility, strength, endurance, edema, perceptual needs, motor planning problems, problem solving, body scheme, and coordination. Functional skills such as dressing, speech, increased self-confidence, risk taking, and socializing are addressable goals for children while enjoying the sensation of water. (Maxine 1998)

- **Water fends off dehydration.**

  Although it has no nutrients, water is essential to health. Water aids digestion, helps prevent constipation, and is vital for proper blood circulation. Children need the same amount of water as an adult: about one quart for every one thousand calories expended. Water also maintains electrolyte balance and is especially important in the summer when heatstroke and heat exhaustion are more likely. Not all children enjoy the taste of water, so diluting juices can help.

  Make it a point to offer water breaks to an extra busy child. Look into using allotted school monies for a classroom water cooler or, better yet, raise the money through a car wash.

Busy Bag Trick
Wrap classroom water bottles in socks to soak up perspiration. Pack eight-ounce water bottles in Keep 'Em Busy bags.

Water Play Possibilities

Extra busy children may enjoy these supervised water play experiences:

Painting Pavement or a Wooden Fence: Put food coloring in the water bucket, and use paintbrushes of all sizes. Hardware stores have sponge brushes that make great paintbrushes for extra busy children. Old pastry, shaving, and makeup brushes are usable too.

Shaking Feathers: Fill a wading pool or large tub with water. Give the extra busy child a few feather dusters to dip and shake.

Blasting Balls: Fill a tub or wading pool with water. Throw a variety of balls inside—ping-pong, tennis, bouncy, or Koosh.

Give the child different-sized turkey basters to blast the balls.

Playing Freely: Fill water tables or tubs with shovels, spoons, strainers, sponges, shells, and empty containers. Let the child play freely in the water. Add food coloring to the water if you like.

Absorbing Water: Fill a wading pool or tub with water. Let the child have a variety of materials: terry cloth, netting, panty hose, sponges, silk, velvet, or a clean diaper. This activity will get an extra busy child's thinking wheels turning. Get ready for questions.

Bathing Bird: Let an extra busy child splash in a clean bird bath with bubbles frothing inside. (Buy a plastic bird bath specifically for bubble play. Clean and cover it after each use.) Here is the basic bubble recipe I use for bird bath play: add about 2 tablespoons dish soap to a cup of water, add more water and glitter or food coloring for flare.

Beating Bubbles: Fill a large bucket with water and a few teaspoons of dish soap. Give the extra busy child an egg beater or whisk for beating bubbles.

Chasing Colored Cubes: New Mexico can serve up some hot summer days. Bella enjoys having colored ice cubes thrown into her wading pool on especially hot ones. I give her a small bug net so she can try to scoop them up before they melt.

Washing Toys: Wash down bicycles, scooters, or dolls with a big bucket of soapy water. Use oversized sponges and lots of suds. Feeling adventurous? Wash the car together.

Playing in Puddles: From thrift stores, purchase several pairs of old galoshes. Make big puddles with a hose (if they are not already supplied by rain) for extra busy children to slosh through. Hand out several plungers specifically set aside for puddle play. Feeling extra brave? Add dirt and have the children mix up mud with only their galoshes.

Share with parents that splashing in the bathtub with toys, colored bath foam, or bubbles is simple water play. When washing a busy child's hair, put an extra drop or two of shampoo in for excess lathering. Go wild with bubble hairdos—spikes, soft-serve ice cream cone curlicues, mohawks, or pigtails. Of course, hand the child a hand mirror for a few giggles.

Keeping a Beach Ball in the Air: Fill a wading pool with water and a couple teaspoons of bath bubbles. Use a water hose to bring the bubbles to life. Pairs can play beach volleyball with the pool acting as a net. The object of the game is to keep the ball and yourself from falling into the water.

Hunting: Fill a tub or wading pool with extra bubbles. Toss several small objects that sink into the water. Have the child hunt for them.

Squirting: Fill up several squirt bottles with water. Let children squirt each other.

Dumping: Extra busy children, especially toddlers, love to dump bottles filled with water. Fill several and watch in amazement.

Filling or Racing Balloons: Fill up mini water balloons to play catch or enjoy water balloon races.

Books

Busy Bag Trick

Ask an extra busy child, "Will you please read a book to me out loud?" Have a childhood or class favorite ready, preferably one with captivating illustrations.

One of the greatest gifts you can offer an extra busy child is a love for reading. Some extra busy children have a natural love for books. Bella is one of these children. She often hops and skips around the house with book in hand. Other extra busy children wouldn't mind if books didn't exist. They are easily frustrated if they have a hard time focusing, avoiding distraction, or sitting still long enough to get through the first few pages. Fortunately, such obstacles can be overcome, and a desire to read can be lavished on extra busy children.

Ideas for Teaching a Love for Reading

Model reading. Extra busy children won't ponder the pleasure of reading if they never see their parents, educators, or caregivers doing it. If a child sees you reading regularly, he'll develop a taste for it. Find time to read in front of extra busy children.

Another highly motivational way to encourage extra busy children to develop a love for reading is to spend time with them engaged in interactive reading, or read-alouds. A formal definition of a "read-aloud" is "the reading of books out loud with the use of expression, different voices for different characters, gestures, and the active participation of the listener through predicting, discussion, and checking for understanding" (Herrell and Jordan 2004, 27). When children see an adult reading confidently to them and with enthusiasm, they want to pick up the same book and read it in the same way. We've all seen this form of mimickry from young children at some time. It's also been clearly demonstrated in my teaching experiences (and with Bella) that children who are interactively read to regularly speak and write better and have much bigger and better vocabularies.

The following are effective steps for interactive reading with an extra busy child:

1. Choose an age-appropriate and attention span–appropriate book, preferably one of interest and slightly above the instructional level of the child.

2. Set aside a time each day when you can read to the child aloud interactively. Remember, interactive reading is exceptional for limited space play and musical movement. (You can bring interactive stories to life through dance.)

3. When possible, read the book ahead of time. Make notes for interactive discussion, posing questions the child might be able to relate to or is currently grappling with at home or at school.

4. Finally, while reading the story, stop and interact within its pages, preferably those most amusing to the busy child. "Look at the bunny in this picture. It looks like our class's pet rabbit. How is it like our rabbit?" Read with enthusiasm, using facial expressions, gestures, and voice variation. End the story with questions that will enhance understanding. "What did you like most about the story?" Ask the child to paraphrase the story. "What was the story about?"

(Herrell and Jordan 2004)

Strengthening the Home-School Connection

For preschoolers and toddlers, encourage their parents to leave books lying around the house on tables, on shelves, and even on the floor.

Busy Bag Trick

To get a must-move-to-learn student or child interested and craving books even more try

- offering fiction and nonfiction books,
- placing books at the child's eye level, and
- visiting the library often for story time.

Strengthening the Home-School Connection

Let parents know that story time is an important part of their extra busy child's bedtime routine. Also, suggest keeping books in a pillowcase in the car, which can entice a child to read. And here's another fabulous book idea to offer parents: Use small books as invitations to parties. Simply punch a hole at the top of the cover and attach a handwritten note to it with string or ribbon.

Always make books readily available to an extra busy child, even before she can read. If you are worried about toddling hands ruining pages, buy sturdy board books. Remember that a toddler's attention span is not long, so keep the books short, colorful, and concise. Make a large selection of books available. Offer not only favorite story books, but also

- beginning reader books such as those by Dr. Seuss;
- simple concept books illustrating numbers, colors, animals, or opposites;
- poetry books;
- senses books that have the child scratch and sniff or feel a textured fabric, pull a tab, or turn the page for the next pop-up picture;
- musical books that play tunes when opened;
- children's magazines like *Your Big Backyard, Ranger Rick, National Geographic Kids,* or *Highlights* (*Highlights* also offers *Highlights High Five,* which is especially for two- to six-year-olds);
- teacher-made books (such as baggie books made from several resealable plastic bags) or memory picture books (made by the child); and
- flannel board stories ("Goldilocks and the Three Bears" is a simple flannel board story to make out of felt).

Support an extra busy child's interests through reading. If an extra busy one loves superheroes, check out several books featuring those characters. If a child would rather read about dolls and pets, find some books about those things. Children often become attached to one particular book or series. This is beneficial because they become acquainted with the words and learn by memorizing. It's also advantageous to give an extra busy child variety. The fresh words and pictures keep children excited about reading. The goal is helping kinesthetic children to want to read and assisting them in seeing the value in it. By making reading exciting and kinesthetically alluring, you will encourage a child to grow up wanting to read books for pure enjoyment.

Make an inviting reading spot available. An extra busy child is more likely to gravitate toward books if the reading space is pleasing to his kinesthetic eye. Put out big fluffy pillows or a huge comforter. I've even seen old bath tubs stuffed with cushions for lounging and reading pleasure in classrooms.

Resources to Jump-Start Your Classroom Read-Alouds

Tell It Again! 2: Easy-to-Tell Stories with Activities for Young Children by Rebecca Isbell and Shirley C. Raines (2000)

All About Pockets: Storytime Activities for Early Childhood by Christine Petrell Kallevig (1993)

Boxes for Play

I think you will agree that children often find boxes more interesting then the items that came in them. There is nothing quite as appealing to a busy mover than an oversized, decorated, comfy box. Boxes can be transformed into a reading refuge and so much more.

Boxes can become special, imaginative safe havens for chilling out, reading, napping, or igniting the imagination. Boxes of all sizes are great for indoor and outdoor inspired and constructive play. The following are a few ideas for turning an ordinary box into an extraordinarily adventurous reading or playing area:

Beach Box: Fill a low-sided box with a small amount of sand. Add a few measuring cups and spoons for an indoor beach adventure. I recommend putting a drop cloth down.

Body Box: A body box is one that appears as if it were made just for the child; he fits snugly inside. Bella has had several body boxes she enjoyed hiding in with blankets and books after a long swimming session. Fill a body box with packing peanuts and let the child sit inside and play. You'll need to supervise well, of course.

Box Bowling: Along with a tennis ball, several shoe boxes (or any similar in size) can muster up a creative game of bowling.

Buildings: Large boxes can become a variety of buildings for learning center play: grocery store, playhouse, post office, fire station, or hospital. Stock each play building with matching supplies—for example, a cash register, play money, and plastic food items for the grocery store.

Camp Out: Turn a big box into a tent. Roll out a sleeping bag. Pack a lunch. Add a flashlight!

Cars: Transform a dryer box into a school bus, fire truck, or a race car.

Caves: After cutting an entryway, give an extra busy child a flashlight so she can explore in the pretend cavern. Drape a blanket over the box for an added cave effect. Or cut a big hole in the top for a submarine effect.

Playhouses: Refrigerator boxes make fabulous playhouses. Cut out a door and windows. Add rooms to the house with a few blankets thrown over several kitchen chairs. Oversized pillows or couch cushions make convenient walls. What about a playhouse turned into a barn? Be imaginative.

Tunnels: Connect a few sturdy boxes together. Drape comforters over the top; the weighted blankets will secure the boxes during movement inside.

Busy Bag Trick
Remove all staples and tape from boxes. Adults should always do the cutting on boxes. Scatter topical books among box play areas.

In Closing . . .

Before diving into chapter 5, remember that nothing characterizes childhood more than play and movement, especially for the kinesthetic child. Extra busy children are intensely curious about their world, and they require daily doses of focused play to explore it. There are numerous ways to serve up play: constructively with creative things, physically in the natural world, or musically in a classroom, to name only a few. Play is a kinesthetic child's learning laboratory, and it is our job as educators to keep this laboratory well stocked with imaginative materials and activities to fuel play that benefits the child academically, socially, and emotionally.

For further play possibilities to enrich an extra busy child's daily schedule, check out these books:

Play: The Pathway from Theory to Practice by Sandra Heidemann and Deborah Hewitt (2010)

Nature in a Nutshell for Kids: Over 100 Activities You Can Do in Ten Minutes or Less by Jean Potter (1995)

I Love Dirt! 52 Activities to Help You and Your Kids Discover the Wonders of Nature by Jennifer Ward (2008)

Don't forget to add these resources to your Busy Bag and suggest them to your students' parents!

There are children playing in the
streets who could solve some
of my top problems in physics,
because they have modes of sensory
perception that I lost long ago.
—J. ROBERT OPPENHEIMER

5

Sensory Integration and Extra Busy Kinesthetic Children

"Sensory integration" is defined as "neurological organization of our senses, like vision, hearing, taste, smell, and touch" (Kranowitz 1992, 25). Sensory integration "is the foundation for moving, learning, speaking, and interacting with the environment" (Kranowitz 1992, 26). It is a tremendous teaching tool for extra busy children.

I became interested in using sensory integration—combining of all major senses to enhance learning—soon after I started teaching in a self-contained, multi-impaired, special needs classroom with several extra busy children. At the time, I was in graduate school facing the selection of a topic for my thesis. I chose sensory-integrated teaching and set up a two-year study, approved by my school district and the university, to determine the effectiveness of implementing a structured, sensory-integrated teaching approach with a small group of elementary-aged students with multiple disabilities in a self-contained classroom. The program design involved several components, including the use of all five senses; eight learning modalities; an intensely structured, predictable classroom management plan; and an incentive-based management program.

Although not a grand-scale study, the significant gains and progress demonstrated by my kinesthetic-natured students with special needs over those two years was enough to alter my overall teaching philosophy and methods.

Currently, I am an adjunct English instructor at a community college. On Sundays, I work with kindergarteners at our family's church. I sensory integrate all of my lessons for all age groups. One of the most encouraging comments I received from a first-year composition student was "Reading the essays aloud in class really helps me. It just helps the material stick better and longer. I haven't read aloud in class since grade school."

An extra busy child's learning potential is optimized with sensory-integrated activities served up in an attractive and engaging environment. This chapter encompasses sensory-integrated play in the form of art and learning activities that can redirect, organize, and capitalize on an extra busy child's nature and routines. The activities overlap in play potential and variety. There are activities for water, outdoor, constructive, and physical play. All are suitable for any time of the day to amuse, enrich, or redirect extra busy children through sensory experiences. The ideas and activities are simple and inexpensive. The supplies needed are easily accessible and more than likely on hand already. The activities can also prove helpful for alleviating extra busy tendencies and catapulting play possibilities.

Sixty-Seven Sensory Play and Art Activities

Even with all of my experience and knowledge about little Bella, it continued to perplex me that although she is bursting with movement 90 percent of the time, she can sit still, completely engrossed in a lengthy feature film. I've concluded that the multisensory experience of the film—sight, sound, and constant screen movement coming at her full speed—mesmerizes her, subduing her kinesthetic nature.

Think again about the meaning of "kinesthetic." (Look back to page 25 for the definition if you like.) Extra busy children are naturally drawn to multisensory, hands-on experiences because that kind of experience fuels their kinesthetic beings and keeps their little clocks ticking. The upcoming pages list sensory-integrated, hands-on play and art activities to use with extra busy children. Share the ideas with others. Remember, you're not alone in extra energy–channeling endeavors. I suggest rotating through the list, not overusing any one activity. I also recommend engaging in the activities with the child the first time around to allow for modeling of appropriate practice, cleaning up, and transitioning.

A Few Important Notes

You'll instantly notice that the alphabetized activities are basically stated. After looking closely at a child's formula for ticking (refer back to the questionnaire in chapter 1), build on the exercises to challenge a child's kinesthetic blueprint. Considering the age appropriateness of each exercise is crucial for the child's learning process too. An extra busy child's skills can be delayed, and they can develop rapidly. If the activity is too simple, she will become easily bored and look for other ways to entertain herself (usually with a busy habit). If the exercise is too advanced, she may play inappropriately, get easily discouraged, or otherwise gain very little from the experience.

As always, keep the activities in the context of age-appropriate safety; a two-year-old shouldn't play in a pretend office center with paper clips and staples. Regarding supplies, fingerpaint can be replaced with any of the substances in the Goopy, Gooey Busyness section of this chapter. A drawing utensil can be a pencil, pen, crayon, marker, colored pencil, or paintbrush. Once again, always consider age appropriateness. Loose-leaf paper, printer paper, construction paper, tag board, origami paper, or cardstock will do for any of the paper exercises. I suggest offering a variety. Continually giving a child white paper when other fabulous colors are available defeats the sensory-integrated purpose. Be resourceful and imaginative.

Apple Printing: Cut an apple in half horizontally, making the center star visible. Place a small amount of fingerpaint in a paint tray. (Old sectioned baby plates, ice cube trays, or muffin tins work well as paint trays.) To print, dip the apple halves in the paint, and press the apple down flat on paper.

Bag Play: Place several objects—such as a mitten, crayon, plastic spoon, eraser, and watch—inside a small paper bag or pillowcase. Teach the child to see with his hands by having him close his eyes, feel an object, and guess what it is as he pulls it out of the bag. Fruit with contrasting textures—like kiwi, peaches, and apples—make interesting mystery bag objects. Another paper bag play activity is to make costumes, such as a set of wings or a suit of armor, out of large brown paper bags. You can also make puppets out of a few bags. Use buttons for eyes, yarn for hair, and bold-colored markers for any final facial decorations.

Ball Play: Fill a box or plastic crate with various balls, such as a basketball, a volleyball, a football, a wiffle ball, and a tennis ball. I do not recommend golf balls, baseballs, or anything an extra busy hand may be tempted to toss aggressively. Grab a ball, go outside, and play catch with a busy child in the fresh air when the climate becomes tense inside the house.

Band Play: Make homemade instruments for a marching band:
Guitars—tissue boxes with rubber bands strapped across the
  top
Maracas—plastic bottles with rocks secured inside
Tambourines—paper plates stapled together with beans or
  rice inside
Drums—oatmeal boxes or big butter tubs
Cymbals—two metal pot lids
Shakers—plastic jars, paper bags, or butter tubs filled with
  rice with the lids on tight.

Let small busy bees jingle and jangle keys. Milk jugs with a few pebbles inside are great noise makers too. March around the house with the child to musical suggestions found later in this chapter. Vary speeds as you march—super slow, super fast, medium slow, very slow, or as fast as you can.

Beads and Buttons: The focus of this activity is beading and stringing patterns. The use of small manipulatives such as beads and buttons is outstanding for enhancing fine

Busy Bag Trick
A child's body can make a variety of sounds to add to band play. He can whistle, hum, sing, snap his fingers, clap his hands, stomp his feet, slap his thighs, rub his hands together, click his tongue, blow raspberries, or pop his cheek.

motor skills for extra busy children. Have an organized assortment for the child. I suggest using an old fishing tackle box to house beads and buttons. Older children can make friendship bracelets or necklaces using thick yarn, twine, string, or thread.

Bean Bag Play: Do you recall carnival bean bag toss games? Make an extra busy child one of her own. Cut four or five holes in the side of a sturdy box. Paint the game box with her, letting her do as much as you see fit. Slant the box or lay it down flat. Toss small bean bags at the holes. You can buy bean bags or make them out of old socks stuffed with beans and sewn shut.

Blow Painting: Place desired amounts of fingerpaint on paper. Give the child a straw to blow designs in the paint. Add different colors for variety. I don't recommend this activity for any extra busy child three or under.

Braiding: Give the child two contrasting pipe cleaners/chenille stems to twist and intertwine. Move on to braiding three after mastering two. Chenille stems can also be shaped into objects like flowers or bracelets. Let him make shapes such as a circle, triangle, square, rectangle, diamond, or heart. Taping yarn pieces down on a table top is also appropriate for teaching children to braid. Feeling brave? Let a child brush and braid your hair (if it's long enough).

Bubble Play: End-of-summer sales have wands and inexpensive crank blowers of different shapes and sizes. Bulk-size liquid bubbles can be acquired at very low prices too. Twisted pipe cleaners/chenille stems make great wands. Bubble blowing isn't limited to warm weather. Try *winter* bubble blowing. When it's brisk enough, bubbles freeze, sparkle, and even bounce when hitting the ground—awesome to observe!

Can Play: Gather a variety of empty, clean metal cans including soup, tuna, coffee, or condensed milk. Remove the labels.

Busy Bag Trick

For all metal or plastic can play, put tape over the rough edges that were made when the lid was removed. I suggest using duct tape.

Give the child a spoon so he can discover the variety of sounds the different cans make when turned upside down.

Carpet Play: Carpet and flooring stores often offer carpet remnants to educators for free or at thrifty prices. Lay down several small carpet pieces in a path around the room. Let the child jump up and down along the handmade trail. Add music.

Cereal Play: String oat loops into bracelets or necklaces. Paint the homemade jewelry. Use different Chex cereals to create a pattern train, such as rice, wheat, corn; rice, wheat, corn. Puffed rice cereals work well for art projects too. Remind children not to eat their beautifully painted cereal projects.

Clay with Cookie Cutters: Purchase an assortment of cookie cutters. Sales after holidays are best for acquiring a variety. Whip up a batch of edible clay using the recipe found later in this chapter. Use the cookie cutters and flat objects, such as lids, the sides of blocks, or spatulas, to make shapes in the clay. Encourage the use of plastic knives, spatulas, or pizza cutters for clay cutting.

Coffee Filter Folding: Give a child several sturdy coffee filters (flimsy ones do not work as well). Have her fold simple shapes, such as triangles, squares, diamonds, and rectangles. Try more advanced shapes, including a pentagon or trapezoid. Have the child fold a filter accordion style and then color the pleats in a pattern with crayons. Coffee filter folding is a quick and easy Keep 'Em Busy bag activity.

Collages: Let a child cut out pictures from old magazines or newspaper ads using a variety of scissors with different edges. Hobby stores carry several types, including wavy and jagged. Glue pictures to heavy construction paper or cardstock. Focus the cutting with directions, such as "Cut only red pictures" or "Cut only objects starting with T." Enhance collages by gluing fabric, wallpaper patches, noodles, popcorn, rice, egg shells (dyed or not), cotton, or tissue paper to them.

Busy Bag Trick

Make a pizza or other scented collage. Seasonings can pack a powerful sensory punch in collages. Try a variety: cilantro leaves, mint flakes, oregano leaves, parsley flakes, shredded lemon peel, bay leaves, sage leaves, poppy seeds, and rosemary leaves. Be sensitive to allergies.

Concentration (a.k.a. Memory): Discount stores have simple, inexpensive, colorful memory games. A deck of cards will work too. Lay all the cards face down and take turns selecting two at a time to acquire sets of the same suit or picture.

Cookie Sheet Play: Gather an assortment of old metal cookie sheets from garage sales. Let a child practice letter identification, create sight words, or spell dictated words with letter magnets. Letter magnets can be purchased inexpensively at discount stores.

Cornmeal Play: Put down a drop cloth or an old sheet. Fill a large bowl or plastic tub with cornmeal. Add spoons of all sizes, miniature cups, or small tea party dishware. Let the child scoop, sift, funnel, and dump the fine substance. Cornmeal play is a great stuck-inside, rainy-day activity. Use oatmeal or grits for variety. Toss in glitter, confetti, rice, sand, dry coffee grounds, or natural materials like bark chunks, pebbles, dry leaves, acorns, grass, hay, or seeds.

Corn on the Cob Printing: After eating a few ears of corn on the cob, set the cobs out in the sun to dry. When completely sun soaked, let the child use a cob as a paint roller with fingerpaint on paper.

Cotton Ball Play: Give a child a bag of cotton balls, glue, and paper. Discount stores carry colored cotton balls for variety. Older extra busy children will take it from there, realizing the rip-ability of cotton. You may need to demonstrate for a younger extra busy child: "Look what I can do with this cotton ball. Can you?"

Cotton Swab Play: Cotton swabs make terrific paintbrushes for young extra busy children. Like cotton balls and craft sticks, a handful of cotton swabs and a bottle of glue can be very entertaining to kinesthetic children. Make star designs or 3-D boxes out of a mound of cotton swabs.

Dominoes: Few children can resist a bucket of old-fashioned dominoes, excellent for constructive play. I also recommend blocks and Legos.

Dot Art: Give a child a marker and paper. Explain that instead of lines he has to use dots to create a picture. After he has dotted a drawing, encourage her to connect her dots.

Egg Play: Decorate and dye hard-boiled eggs anytime. Use corn syrup to stick small candies or sprinkles to the outside. Have an egg hunt in July or September. Stock up on marked-down dye and plastic eggs after Easter.

Feather Play: Hobby stores carry brilliantly colored craft feathers. Let an energetic child sort them or make artistic and imaginative birds or flowers with the feathers, paper, and glue.

Flour Play: Put a sheet down on a lawn. Give the child a sifter, measuring scoops, and a tub of white flour to play in. When done playing, discard the flour and shake off the sheet. Or fill an old oatmeal box with flour. Slice small holes in the plastic lid, and let the child frolic and sprinkle flour about on the ground outdoors. An empty spice container will work too. A passing rain cloud will eventually erase the play.

Foam Play: An old foam mattress can provide toe squishing, hopping, and tumbling pleasure. Teach the child to do somersaults, cartwheels, handstands, and rolls. Search for "memory foam" online for additional ideas.

Hand, Foot, or Body Tracing: This is a quick, hands-on activity. Give the child a piece of paper and a drawing utensil to trace his hands. Have him decorate the hand tracings and cut them out. Hand tracing is excellent fine motor play, especially when the child has to trace with her nondominant hand. Move on to tracing other objects such as feet, puzzle pieces, cookie cutters, and small toys. Rev up the enjoyment by tracing the child's body on a large piece of butcher paper.

Strengthening the Home-School Connection

If a busy bee takes to tumbling, recommend or check into a physical play program especially for toddlers and preschoolers, such as the national program Gymboree (www.gymboreeclasses .com). These programs encourage music, art, and lots of sensory play.

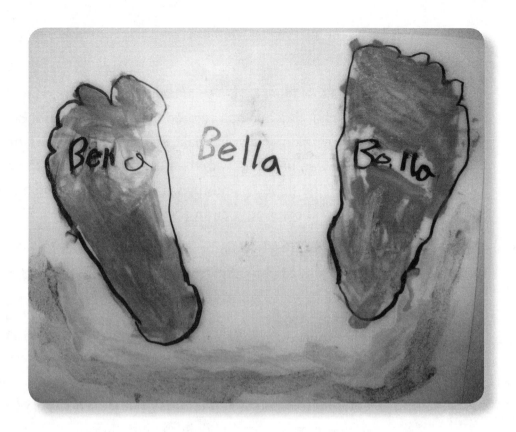

Let him trace yours. Fill in the tracing with clothes and distinguishable body parts. Cut out and display.

Hole Punching: Give a child cardstock and a hole punch for punching out requested designs or shapes. Discount stores have punchers with different hole shapes, such as hearts and other seasonal designs. Hole punching a single sheet of cardstock paper has amused Bella for up to twenty minutes.

Lacing Cards: Lacing cards can be purchased at educational stores or made on your own with colored cardstock or sandpaper (by punching out patterned holes with a hole punch). Get creative with the designs. Shoelaces work best for lacing.

Marble Painting: Put a piece of paper in a shoe box. Add a little paint and a couple of marbles. Secure the lid tightly with tape or hold it closed. Let the child manipulate the box to roll the marble inside. Then open the box for a marbled mystery design.

Marshmallow Play: Give a child several regular marshmallows and a handful of small colored marshmallows too. Have her create objects or animals, such as a snowman, robot, caterpillar, or a dog, with the marshmallows and toothpicks. Using fine-tipped paintbrushes to paint large marshmallows with food coloring is simple and amusing too.

Mirror Play: With a hand mirror, make funny faces together. See if the child can imitate what you do. Extra busy toddlers especially enjoy mirror play.

Mural Play: On a wall or side of a building, put up newspaper or a large old sheet. I suggest covering a substantial section. Give the child a paintbrush and a bowl of water with food coloring to create a mural. Spray bottles work too. Washable tempera paint is another alternative.

Newspaper Play: Using newsprint to entertain extra busy children is versatile and easy. Make hats, wad up several sheets and shoot hoops in the waste basket, or lay a few sheets down and paint directly on them.

Office Play: Set up a mini office area with essential play supplies, such as an old rotary phone, a used computer monitor, pencils, paper, file folders, calculators, paper clips, staplers, hole punches, rubber stamps, and ink pads. An old typewriter will spark an extra busy child's curiosity.

Paper Dolls: Buy paper dolls or make your own with the child out of cardstock. Making and playing with paper dolls enhance fine motor skills. To make them more durable, paint the cut outs with a coat or two of clear nail polish.

Papier-Mâché Play: Flour and water make a messy, wet substance that extra busy children love! Tear old newspapers into strips, soak the strips in the papier-mâché mess, and

Busy Bag Trick

Mirrors are effective tools for helping extra busy children work on identifying their feelings before, in the mist of, or after a busy episode. Give the child a hand mirror and ask, "How are you feeling now?" Or role-play behaviors, such as manners or waiting patiently for assistance, while in front of a mirror.

cover a balloon thoroughly with the wet strips. Or just let the child play in the mucky sensory mess. I suggest putting down several old sheets on the floor.

Paper Tearing: When Bella is being especially stubborn and busy, I give her a piece of newspaper to tear into strips. Step the activity up a level by tearing it into even smaller pieces for gluing a design.

Making a rainbow fish is an enjoyable paper-tearing activity. Cut a fish shape out of cardstock. If the child is able, have him divide the fish into seven sections—one for each color of the rainbow (red, orange, yellow, green, blue, indigo, and violet). He can glue torn colored paper pieces to each section. Culminate the activity by reading a book from the Rainbow Fish series by Marcus Pfister at read aloud time.

Pasta Art: Pasta comes in all shapes and sizes. String it. Paint it. Glue it. Sort it. Count it. Just use it. Turn to page 4 to read about Bella's pasta tub play.

Piñata: Fill a handmade papier-mâché version or a store-bought piñata with packaging peanuts, foam pieces, and a few treats. The whacking is excellent physical play.

Pinecone Play: Have the child gather pinecones outside. Take out a large pot, tub, or box, and have her stand about three feet away to try and make baskets with the gathered pinecones. Make a quick birdfeeder by smearing pinecones with peanut butter and then rolling them in birdseed.

Playdough Pressing: After whipping up a batch of homemade playdough (page 154), let the child press patterns into the dough with a variety of small objects. Use an old waffle iron with the cord cut off, a rolling pin, or a garlic press for pretend kitchen play.

Plunger Play: Purchase several plungers *specifically for play*. Make water puddles outside and let extra busy children plunge away. The suction sound and force on sidewalks or slides is naturally entertaining to kinesthetic children.

Pot and Pan Play: Young extra busy children love pot and pan play. Offer a variety of pan and pot sizes. Complete the music making with wooden spoons.

Potato Prints: Instead of apples, use potatoes for printing on paper with fingerpaint. For variety, give the child an old potato masher to dip in paint for printing interesting designs.

Potting Soil Play: Fill a large plastic planting pot with potting soil. Give the child a hodgepodge of safe tools. I don't recommend this activity for indoors—save it for outside. Provide little pots or paper cups for him to use for planting bean seeds in the soil to enhance the activity.

Pudding Play: Use pudding as you would fingerpaint on paper. Vanilla pudding with a drop or two of food coloring can make interesting colors. Remind extra busy children not to share their pudding and to wash their hands before eating or licking.

Puppets: Turn old socks into puppets. Use markers to draw a funny face. Add hair and clothes. Teach an older child to sew on buttons. Put a box up for a puppet show. You can use paper plates on tongue depressors for puppets. Broken peanut shells make quick finger puppets. (The steps are simple: Break the peanut shell and eat the peanuts inside. Fit half of a shell on an index finger and decorate it with thin-tipped markers.) Other puppet ideas include plastic- or wooden-spoon puppets, envelope puppets, toilet-paper-tube puppets, and conventional paper-sack puppets.

Puzzle Play: Puzzles are terrific for honing concentration skills, and they come in many varieties, such as magnetic, wooden, textured, or 3-D. Our family enjoys puzzle races. Garage sales practically give them away. Age-appropriateness is pertinent here.

Rainbow Art: Anything demonstrating and reinforcing the ROYGBIV concept (red, orange, yellow, green, blue, indigo, violet) in a spectrum design is considered rainbow art. Colored cereal pieces glued accordingly is an easy rainbow activity. Stringing a rainbow pattern with beads or colored pasta is one option. See the paper tearing activity in this section for a rainbow fish idea.

Rock Painting: Let a child gather rocks of different shapes and sizes. She can paint them outside on newspaper or at a covered table. Washable tempera paint is best for this activity. Reinforce the seriousness of rock throwing and the correspondingly severe consequences for choosing to do so during this activity.

Rubbings: Place flat objects under a piece of paper. Using the side of a crayon or piece of chalk, rub back and forth over the items. Sandpaper, leaves, paper clips, keys, and various

Busy Bag Trick

To enhance a rock painting activity, have children first sort the rocks by size, texture, color, or shape before painting. Other rock and rock-related ideas include

- polishing rocks with sandpaper
- using rocks in paper rubbings
- turning a rock into a pet
- sifting and panning for gold-painted rocks in a large tub of water
- making rock candy (children love watching crystals form!)
- using rock salt to make ice cream.

coins are quality rubbing materials. Move rubbings outside. Tape large pieces of paper to trees and let children rub away.

Shadow Play: With the child, lie on the floor with a flashlight. Make sure the lights are off or fairly dim. With your hands in the light, make shadow puppets. Tell stories. Add soft music.

Sink or Float Sort: Fill a large tub with water. Label two small containers "sink" and "float." Give the child several objects that either sink or float, allowing him to place the objects in each container accordingly after testing. Although some may raise an eyebrow, I think this activity is suitable for extra busy children as small as two years of age. The concept will get their little thinking wheels chugging. Activities involving standing water should always be supervised.

Sponge Painting: Instead of apples or potatoes, use sponges. Offer a variety of shapes and sizes. Use very porous sponges and not-so-porous sponges. Use fingerpaint, pudding, mud, or tempera paint for sponge painting.

Stencils and Stamps: Hobby stores have vast collections of stencils, stamps, and colored ink pads. Make your own stencils with cardstock. Little thumbs make fabulous natural stamps.

Sticker Play: Children love bright stickers. As an extra busy child, I enjoyed scratch-and-sniff stickers. Buy several packages of dime-sized ones. Dispense half a sheet at a time for play on paper. Draw circles on paper for the child to practice one-to-one correspondence. "Place one sticker inside each circle." Bella's pediatrician recommended www.mrsgrossmans.com for stickers galore.

Tissue Play: Buy several boxes of inexpensive tissues. When a young kinesthetic child is restless, give him a full box and allow him to pull the tissues out one by one and frolic in them. Bella loved this activity as a toddler—still does! Wet wipes work well too.

Tongs Play: Gather several small items, such as cotton balls, marbles, or tiny toys. Give the child a large pair of kitchen tongs and let her transfer the items from one big bowl to another. This is excellent fine motor play. Alternatively, use a cupcake or jumbo muffin pan for sorting objects.

Top Play: Tops are tops! Buy a variety of sizes for a child to spin. Encourage her to spin several at a time.

Tortilla Art: Give the child a warm tortilla to use as paper and two teaspoons of melted butter in a dish with a smidgen of food coloring and milk as his paint. Let him use a brand new paintbrush to create a yummy snack. Wash the paintbrush and store it for future food use only. Toast works as paper too.

Tube Talking: Purchase an assortment of inexpensive plastic tubing from a hardware store. Place pieces in a bin. Let the child experiment with the sounds of blowing, humming, and talking into the different sized tubes. Or connect several clear tubes for whooshing small items through.

Wax Paper Painting: Place a desired amount of fingerpaint on a piece of paper. Lay a piece of wax paper over the top. Let the child doodle, draw, or design patterns and pictures with her hands or a drawing or cooking utensil. Remove the wax paper from the top for a finished design.

Whiffing: Place several distinct foods with obvious smells in plastic cups: vinegar, vanilla, lemon, peppermint, mayonnaise, and onion soup mix work well. Have the child close his eyes and try to identify the odors.

Window Art: New Mexico's summertime heat can be unbearable for midday outdoor play. As the temperature drops in the evening hours, Bella enjoys decorating the patio window with cling art (from holiday sales), fingerpaint, or washable window markers. She also enjoys erasing her work with the water hose.

Busy Bag Trick
Tables covered with sheets give obstacle courses an imaginative tunnel effect.

Wood Walking: Obtain a piece of flat, smooth plywood to act as a walking beam or balancing board. Cover it with electrical tape to keep little feet splinter free. Connect several boards for enhanced play. Step the energy level up by having the child balance on the beam while walking sideways, backward, or with her hands behind her back. Put objects between the boards for her to maneuver through, or turn the activity into a full-fledged obstacle course with pillows to jump on or chairs to crawl in and out of.

Additional Resources for Sensory Play and Art Activities

ArtStarts for Little Hands! Fun and Discoveries for 3- to 7-Year-Olds
    by Judy Press (2000)
The Mudpies Book of Boredom Busters by Nancy Blakey (1999)
The Big Messy Art Book by MaryAnn F. Kohl (2000)

Goopy, Gooey Busyness

Nothing puts a bigger smile on most extra busy children's faces like playing with goopy, gooey substances. You'll soon discover how clay and dough are effective fidget materials. Goopy, gooey fidget and play experiences can be easily sensory-integrated for an extra busy child. For example, make playdough edible and add vanilla or peppermint extract to make it smell good.

Be aware though—not *all* extra busy children share the pleasure of goopy, gooey messes. I have worked with children who refuse to get their little hands messy with icky stuff. For these cautious children, I recommend spray bottles, frosting tubes, sponges, spatulas, glue sticks, or old squeezable mustard or ketchup containers to use for manipulating, squeezing, poking at, or stirring up messy materials. Using rubber gloves or tight fitting surgical ones to play in wet materials can also create a sensory experience like no other for kinesthetic children.

The following goopy, gooey sensory substances are for an extra busy child to enjoy, in and out of the classroom. The recipes are simple, fast, and sure to please when extra busy habits need to be quickly redirected, appeased through play, or occupied during time in limited spaces. As always, keep safety and allergies in mind.

Edible Clay

> 1/2 cup butter (1 stick)
> 1/2 cup corn syrup (light or dark)
> 1 tablespoon salt
> 4 cups powdered sugar

Mix the ingredients together for a mushy, moldable, edible clay. Depending on the texture you desire, add more or less powdered sugar.

Easy Goop

> 1 16 oz. box of cornstarch
> water (according to desired consistency)
> food coloring (optional)

Mix the cornstarch and water to the desired consistency. Add food coloring if you like.

Lickable Fingerpaint

> 1/2 cup flour
> 2 cups water, plus 4 tablespoons
> 2 tablespoons cornstarch
> food coloring

Mix the flour and 2 cups of water in a pan. Simmer, stirring constantly. In a bowl, mix cornstarch with 4 tablespoons of cold water; stir this into the simmering flour mixture. Let cool and color with small amounts of food coloring. I discard the mix after each use.

Easiest Fingerpaint Ever

1 can condensed milk
food coloring

Mix condensed milk with food coloring. Add sensory value by tossing in rice, sand, peppermint extract, and crayon shavings. Explain to children that the substance is not lickable.

Gunk

1 cup school glue
food coloring
1 tablespoon liquid starch

Mix together the glue, a few drops of food coloring, and the liquid starch. Keep it at the table on a tray. It's gunky, messy, sticky, but sooooo much fun.

Simple Playdough

3 cups flour
1/2 cup vegetable oil
1/2 cup water
food coloring (optional)
almond, vanilla, lemon, or peppermint extract (or others; optional)

Mix the ingredients and knead well. Add food coloring and/or scented flavorings.

Yummy Playdough

1/4 cup peanut butter
1 tablespoon honey
3 tablespoons powdered milk

Mix ingredients and knead until sticky. Put in refrigerator to chill for about 20 minutes before use.

Busy Bag Trick

Store playdough in airtight resealable containers or bags. Never leave it in a hot area. I recommend using each batch of homemade playdough only once—germs galore. Add sand, oatmeal, glitter, confetti, or food coloring for variety and texture. Almond, lemon, and vanilla extracts are fabulous additions too, especially in the Yummy Playdough recipe.

Pretend Snow

Instant snow is an inexpensive, nontoxic, fluffy, wet indoor wonder. Search for instant snow activities online.

    2 cups white powdered laundry detergent
    1/2 cup water

Combine in a blender or whip with an electric mixer until doughy. Toss in some glitter or confetti for extra excitement. Enhance snow activities by giving a child a spray bottle full of colored water to color the snow.

Pretzel Dough

Making pretzel dough, forming a pretzel, baking a pretzel, and eating a pretzel is a terrific sequencing and attention-building skill for extra busy children.

    2 cups flour
    1 teaspoon sugar
    1 teaspoon honey
    2 teaspoons dry yeast
    3/4 cup warm water
    toppings, such as melted butter with cinnamon, salt,
      or sprinkles

Mix together yeast and warm water. Combine the yeast mixture with the remaining ingredients in a large bowl. Knead for 10 to 15 minutes. Form into 6-8 medium-size pretzel shapes. Bake at 350 degrees for 10 minutes. Cool. Use pastry brushes to paint on a little melted butter. Sprinkle with cinnamon or a few sprinkles.

Pudding: Instant, cooked, or premade pudding makes a quick, delicious paint. Bella loves pudding painting to this day—she's not as messy as she used to be though. Refer to page 148 for pudding play.

Silly Putty: Discount stores carry Silly Putty at reasonably low prices and usually in old-fashioned plastic eggs. It's great for Keep 'Em Busy bags. The Gunk recipe above can be modified to make Silly Putty by increasing the glue and decreasing the liquid starch.

Whipping Cream: Whipping cream play works best on clean cookie sheets or vinyl tablecloths. Bella's extra busy little fingers still enjoy sneaking a taste or two. Add food coloring or dry Kool-Aid for flare.

Yogurt: Yogurt mixed with raisins, sunflower seeds, or granola makes a sensational textured substance for smearing on construction or wax paper.

Coffee Grounds: Used coffee grounds (wet or dry) mixed with uncooked rice or grits is an awesome sensory play substance. Let a child play with the grounds on wax paper or in a tub with scoops and cups.

Mashed Potatoes: Really! Leftover mashed potatoes can be easily turned into a usable goopy, gooey play substance for kinesthetic children to manipulate on wax paper or a cookie sheet. Add water to thin out the spuds or wheat germ to thicken them. The objective is to make the potatoes as sensory-stimulating to the hands and eyes as possible. Add coconut, frozen raisins, frozen peas, or sunflower seeds. Inedible additions are wonderful too. Try small beads, colored sand, or squishy packing peanuts. Discard after use.

More Goopy, Gooey Ideas

To expand your goopy, gooey recipe collection for your Keep 'Em Busy Bag check out the following books:

Make Your Own Playdough, Paint, and Other Craft Materials: Easy Recipes to Use with Young Children by Patricia Caskey (2006)

Pure Slime: 50 Incredible Ways to Make Slime Using Household Substances by Brian Rohrig (2004)

Glues, Brews, and Goos: Recipes and Formulas for Almost Any Classroom Project by Diane F. Marks (1996)

Music and Movement

Music combined with creative movement plays an essential part in a balanced approach to nurturing a kinesthetic nature. Putting movement to music naturally increases learning potential and focus for many extra busy children. Creative musical movement also aids in developing social and cognitive skills. Moving musical experiences also pave an avenue for extraordinary cultural experiences.

Extra busy children are naturally spontaneous, making musical play activities easy to enjoy and welcome in any home or classroom. Playing and learning with the support of music and movement can also help you positively connect to a child's language capabilities, memory, physical activity, creative thinking, emotional stability, discipline, and academic success (Carlton 2000, 1).

Benefits of Using Music and Movement

Here are just a few of the numerous benefits of music and movement for extra busy kinesthetic children.

- **Music helps children listen better.**

  Children naturally tune in to songs and instrumental music. Listen to music and play games by asking, "What is that sound?" "Who is talking/singing?" "What is making that sound?" Games like this encourage children to listen creatively and intentionally (Carlton 2000, 1).

- **Music helps children remember.**

  Music is a great mnemonic learning and teaching device. Songs like "The Hokey Pokey," "This Old Man," and "You Are My Sunshine" all require high levels of memorization and focus, especially with added movements. Putting everyday class or home routines to music can greatly assist an extra busy child's recollection of exact procedures.

- **Music helps children focus.**

  Nursery rhymes with a steady beat encourage children to slow down in word pronunciation and focus on a task. Try a rhythmic round of "Where Is Thumbkin?" with extra busy children to experience how much music can help them speak more clearly and pay closer attention.

- **Music helps children transition.**

  Extra busy children respond more effectively to activity transitioning if it is accompanied by a delightful singing of "Clean up! Clean up! Time to put things away!" instead of "Okay, Sonja. Your playtime is over. Put your stuff away."

- **Music helps children think critically.**

  Singing games, action rhymes, and fingerplays catapult children to later problem-solving and memorization skills. Music also keeps children alert for longer projects (Carlton 2000, 4).

Getting Started

A few simple tips will help you add music and movement to an extra busy child's play possibilities. Old-fashioned fingerplays, action rhymes, appropriate musical choices, and imaginative props help make the time fun and meaningful. Music itself encourages learning and redirecting of extra busy habits. The key is to initiate and guide the exercises, not mandate and control them. You merely supply the materials, and a child's kinesthetic nature and curiosity will take it from there.

- Keep musical activities simple and diverse.
- Use props, such as socks, scarves, balloons, and ribbons. See the longer list on page 165.
- Squeeze music in whenever and wherever possible with gross motor movement (physical play).
- Be consistent—continue offering music! Children who are not initially interested will eventually start tapping their tiny toes.
- Never rush. Nobody likes to start and then turn right around and stop, especially children.
- Make sure the music is not jumbled, too loud, or too soft.
- Set clear and consistent environmental musical and movement limits. Examples may include no jumping, no flailing rhythm sticks near other children, and no running in the classroom.

Simple Musical Experiences for Extra Busy Children

"The Itsy Bitsy Spider" is a wonderful example of a childhood favorite fingerplay. Fingerplays and rhymes are fabulous for classroom story time and home experiences, especially bedtime routines. Fingerplays add variety, encourage participation, promote focusing, and are great for getting rid of wiggles after long periods of sitting. Add familiar music or tunes to rhymes and fingerplays. Build a collection of rhymes and fingerplays for your Busy Bag. Teaching, singing, modeling, and participating in various rhymes and fingerplays can prove helpful when extra busy habits become intense. And remember, the more often you use them, the more effective and enjoyable they become.

Below I've listed some favorites from my teaching experiences and playing with my own children. You'll notice the songs aren't new. I grew up with them. You probably did too. These can be used effectively at home, too, so share them with parents.

Body Instruments—a Great Fidget Buster: Have children take a five-minute marching body parade break in the classroom or from homework by turning their bodies into instruments. To be a trombone, children move their arms toward and away from their mouths. They wiggle their fingers from both hands off of one side of their mouth to imitate a flute, or softly pat their stomachs to imitate a drum. March in a step count around the classroom or your house. This is a great one-on-one-time activity for a parent and child.

The Wave—Put to Music: Have children stand shoulder to shoulder with some space between them. Demonstrate the wave. Put your arms high in the air and make a waving motion through your body, starting at your fingertips and ending with your toes. Add groovy music. If one-on-one with a child, stand face-to-face and wave. Teach the children the worm crawl too. Lie on the floor and wiggle your body forward.

Five Little Pumpkins

This one is a fall favorite.

Five little pumpkins sitting on a gate. (One hand up.)
The first one said, "Oh my, it's getting late." (Wiggle thumb.)
The second one said, "There are witches in the air."
   (Wiggle pointer finger.)
The third one said, "But we don't care." (Wiggle middle
   finger.)
The fourth one said, "I'm ready for some fun." (Wiggle fourth
   finger.)
The fifth one said, "Let's run, and run, and run." (Wiggle little
   finger.)
"O-o-o-o-o," goes the wind . . . and out went the lights.
   (Close fingers into fist.)
And the five little pumpkins rolled out of sight. (Open hand
   and wiggle fingers.)

Five Little Monkeys

This is another rendition of "Five Little Pumpkins."

(Hold up five fingers and sing.) *Five little monkeys jumping
   on the bed. One fell off and bumped his head. Mama*

called the doctor and the doctor said, "No more monkeys
jumping on the bed."

(Hold up four fingers and sing.) *Four little monkeys jumping
on the bed. One fell off and bumped his head. Mama
called the doctor and the doctor said, "No more monkeys
jumping on the bed."*

(Repeat, counting down, until there are no little monkeys
left.)

My Bonnie Lies Over the Ocean

I use my hands as ocean waves for this short sing-along.

My Bonnie lies over the ocean.
My Bonnie lies over the sea.
My Bonnie lies over the ocean.
Oh, bring back my Bonnie to me.
Bring back, bring back,
Oh, bring back my Bonnie to me.

Fish

One, two, three, four, five
Once I caught a fish alive.
Six, seven, eight, nine, ten,
Then I let it go again.
Why did you let it go?
Because it bit my finger so.
Which finger did it bite?
This little finger on the right.

Yankee Doodle

This is the basic version. A longer one exists,
but I find keeping it simple works best for extra busy
children.

Yankee Doodle went to town,
Riding on a pony.
He stuck a feather in his hat
And called it macaroni.

Busy Bag Trick

"This Old Man" is a great mnemonic device for extra busy children needing to remember procedures or lists. Reinvent and teach the song as a memory tool with corresponding rhyming words, such as

1 = bun, fun, sun

2 = shoe, do

3 = tree, me, see

4 = door, floor, chore

5 = hive, strive, alive

6 = fix, mix, nix

7 = heaven, eleven

8 = gate, rate, mate

9 = line, fine, dine

10 = when, been, den

Be inventive.

(Chorus)

Yankee Doodle, keep it up,

Yankee Doodle Dandy.

Mind the music and the step

and with the girls be handy.

Baby Bumblebee

This is another one of Bella's favorites.

I'm bringing home a baby bumblebee.

Won't my mommy be so proud of me?

I'm bringing home a baby bumblebee.

"Ouch!" It stung me!

Children like to really ham up the "ouch!" Consider several actions for it.

The Ants Go Marching

This summertime favorite can be accompanied with any hand and foot movements, not necessarily a march.

The ants go marching one by one, hurrah, hurrah.

The ants go marching one by one, hurrah, hurrah.

The ants go marching one by one,

The little one stops to suck his thumb,

And they all go marching down

Into the ground

To get out of the rain.

Boom. Boom. Boom!

It's Raining, It's Pouring

It's raining, it's pouring,

The old man is snoring.

He went to bed and bumped his head

And couldn't get up in the morning.

If You're Happy and You Know It

If you're happy and you know it, clap your hands (clap, clap).

If you're happy and you know it, clap your hands (clap, clap).

If you're happy and you know it, then your face will surely show it,

If you're happy and you know it, clap your hands (clap, clap).

This happy tune has alternate verses including throw a kiss, stomp your feet, touch your nose, twist your hips, and give a hug. You can also add your own.

Old McDonald Had a Farm

This is a traditional favorite for children!

Old McDonald had a farm, E-I-E-I-O.
And on his farm he had some chicks, E-I-E-I-O.
With a chick, chick here and a chick, chick there,
Here a chick, there a chick,
Everywhere a chick chick.
Old McDonald had a farm, E-I-E-I-O.

Add alternate animal sounds such as quack-quack for a duck, moo-moo for a cow, gobble-gobble for a turkey, and oink-oink for a pig! Once again, be creative.

Teddy Bear Teddy Bear

This one is a favorite of smaller children, one to three years of age.

Teddy Bear (clap), *Teddy Bear* (clap), *turn around* (turn around).
Teddy Bear (clap), *Teddy Bear* (clap), *touch the ground* (bend down and touch floor).
Teddy Bear (clap), *Teddy Bear* (clap), *touch the sky* (reach up in the air).

Additional verses include blink your eyes, tap your knees, and toot your horn. Use your imagination!

These are other simple, well-known favorites to try with extra busy children.
- "Patty-Cake"
- "London Bridge Is Falling Down"

- "I'm a Little Teapot"
- "Johnny Works with One Hammer"
- "The Farmer in the Dell"
- "Rain, Rain, Go Away"
- "There Was an Old Lady Who Swallowed a Fly"
- "Are You Sleeping?"
- "Three Little Ducks"
- "Twinkle, Twinkle, Little Star"
- "The Wheels on the Bus"

Good Musical Movement Choices

Like a diverse play menu, a diverse musical menu will greatly benefit extra busy children. For inspiring movement, I find instrumental music is best. Visit a local music store or library to select music that stirs up a desired mood or cultural experience. Use music from a variety of cultures and traditions. There are many kinds of music to choose from: jazz, folk, country, rock, even reggae. The possibilities are endless. Ask children to bring in favorite music varieties from home. I recommend always listening to music prior to playing it for children, especially those sensitive to certain sounds.

Classical

- "Pictures at an Exhibition" and "Night on Bald Mountain" by Modest Mussorgsky
- "The Nutcracker Suite" by Pyotr Ilich Tchaikovsky
- "Peter and the Wolf" by Sergei Prokofiev (This one can be a musical variation on story time.)

Jazz, New Age, and Percussion

- "Between Two Worlds" by Patrick O'Hearn
- "Chameleon Days" by Yanni

- "Nightnoise" by Billy Oskay and Michael O'Domhnail
- "Winter into Spring" by George Winston
- "White Winds" by Andreas Vollenweider
- "Planet Drum" by Mickey Hart

Imaginative Props

With props, children become aware of their bodies and how they work during musical movement. Extra busy children who have trouble participating may suddenly become eager with the security of a music prop in hand. Extra busy children who are especially clumsy, careless, or easily distracted can benefit from using props with musical movement play. Gather props of all shapes, colors, and sizes. Dramatic play items children can wear make awesome props. Let the children choose their own props, and display the props in a big box for easy access during classroom learning center time. Like music, prop possibilities are limitless. The following are examples of fun props. Remember to keep in mind age appropriateness and safety.

- long wooly scarves, bright boas
- sheets, socks, puppets (hand or stick)
- crepe paper streamers, pom-poms, fabric remnants, rolled-up newspapers
- paper fans, flowers, leaves
- hoops (cut the centers out of big plastic coffee can lids) or Hula-hoops
- craft feathers, wings from old costumes, tubes of all sizes for making exaggerated voices
- hats, crowns, caps, dramatic play clothing (shorten to eliminate tripping)
- small hand-held mirrors
- instruments like recorders, castanets, Boomwhackers, sand blocks, harmonicas, rainsticks (see page 140 for homemade instrument ideas)

- Flashlights for musical movement in dim lighting (Bella loves this!)

Finally, remember that extra busy children dance to the beat of a different drum. Let them explore their nature through their musical movement experiences with no questions asked (excluding those about safety, of course).

In Closing . . .

Before moving on to chapter 6, remember this: combining sensory integration with playful and creative art activities is an effective method of enhancing a child's development and nurturing her nature, especially an extra busy child's. And, since making sensory-integrated play exercises successful is largely a matter of approach, delivery to kinesthetic children is easy—simply plug directly into their busyness and unique formula for ticking.

Moreover, as an educator, you have the power to cause an extra busy child to be a successful student. With this in mind, never underestimate the power of the senses when they are combined with play to prompt an extra busy child to take his abilities above and beyond all they dare to be.

For further sensory-integrated ideas, games, and activities for children, extra busy children included, check out these books:

Learning Games: Exploring the Senses through Play by Jackie Silberg (2006)
The Complete Book of Rhymes, Songs, Poems, Fingerplays, and Chants by Jackie Silberg and Pam Schiller (2006)

And don't forget to make room in your Busy Bag for these resources!

6

Whatever they grow up to be, they are still our children, and the one most important of all the things we can give to them is unconditional love. Not a love that depends on anything at all except that they are our children.

—ROSALEEN DICKSON

The Basics of Sleeping and Eating for Extra Busy Kinesthetic Children

As a parent and educator, I think I can safely say that children are most unproductive when they are either tired or hungry. Extra busy children who skip meals (especially breakfast), load up on empty calories, or fall asleep watching the late show are not prepared for a functional day of learning and playing hard at home or school. Extra busy children who eat unbalanced meals and sleep inconsistently are irritable and moody, have trouble concentrating, and usually display heightened extra busy habits.

Nutritious meals and adequate sleep are important in an extra busy child's life. The American Heart Association offers a set of guidelines to follow for nutritiously feeding young children. I suggest looking closely at the recommendations, especially in light of today's supersized meal mentality. The recommendations are easily accessible online at www.americanheart.org.

For a child-friendly food pyramid to display in the classroom and share with families, visit www.mypyramid.gov. Other helpful nutritional Web sites include www.eatright.org and www.nutrition.gov.

I believe a connection exists between what children eat and how they behave. I believe the same can be said for how a child sleeps. This chapter addresses successful food and sleep strategies for an extra busy child. If you are a child care provider, consider using these strategies in your business and sharing them with parents of extra busy children. If you teach school-age children, consider sharing this information with your busy bees' parents. Before digging in, here are the four most common adverse food reactions in children, extra busy children included.

- Gastrointestinal reactions: After eating a select food item a child may experience diarrhea, vomiting, spitting, colic, or a stomachache.
- Skin reactions: A child may react to a food by developing a rash or hives.
- Respiratory reactions: A child may develop a cough, wheezing, or nasal congestion after consuming a food.
- Behavioral changes: A child may experience increased restlessness and irritability after consuming certain foods.

(Kennedy, Terdal, and Fusetti 1993, 29)

The Importance of Proper Food and Sleep

Ben F. Feingold, a prominent pediatrician who specialized in children's allergies, wrote a groundbreaking bestseller in 1975, *Why Your Child Is Hyperactive.* It detailed how a child's behavior could be significantly altered by artificial food coloring and flavoring. The diet that Feingold designed improved the lives of many children worldwide, but it remains challenged by specialists today. A food's ability to charge up or shut down a child remains largely dependent on the system makeup of each individual. What traps one child may free another. Nevertheless, children, especially extra busy children, require a balanced and nutritious diet for proper growth, development, and learning stamina.

Meet Ed

I am tuned in to my food intake and the effect certain foods have on my body as well as my children's. What parent or teacher isn't?

You know when an extra busy child isn't feeling well or hasn't had enough sleep. His actions deviate from normal everyday behavior. The same is true for food consumption. Honestly, I'll disclose that I'm probably borderline obsessive with food attunement. Let me explain.

Somewhere along my adolescent journey I developed an eating disorder. I'll refer to this scoundrel as "Ed." Ed disguised himself as purposeful in the early years of our courtship. I leaned on him to regain my figure quickly after having children. Ed emotionally saw me through graduate school while raising them and assisted my efforts to deal—dangerously—with the onset of severe anxiety after the birth of busy Bella. For years, he punished my body, especially my digestive and nervous systems. I vacillated between triumphs and tribulations for almost two decades before finally realizing my destructive eating habits were slowly destroying me. And they were preventing me from giving my children and students my best.

Looking back, Ed proved to be nothing but a liar—or as Bella would call her big sister, "a real meany-bo-beany!" Sporadic, unhealthy eating made me sluggish, irritable, and flighty. I endured the highest of sugar highs and lowest of crashing-carb lows. Add nursing colicky baby Bella to the equation, and I staved off a straight jacket by a mere electrolyte or two.

Having a Plan of Attack

Food addiction recovery taught me much about the virtue of simplicity, and the power of proper food and exercise for running the body effectively and efficiently—versus haphazardly and dangerously. Your body, the one entrusted with caring for and teaching children, as well as an extra busy child's body, is made of and responds to its fueling substance. I'd like to share a brief story to bring my point to life.

I regularly visit with a girlfriend over coffee. Sometimes we chat at my house, other times, hers. Our busy children play while we spend time together. This particular go around we were at her house. Our children weren't any busier than usual. They were bringing toy vehicles to life with powerful vrooms and zooms. An empty coffee mug sent me to the kitchen, where I was bombarded with all sorts of available goodies—a glass cookie jar stocked full to the lid, a bag of potato chips clipped shut next to the blender, a box of donut holes nestled next to the toaster, and a half-eaten store cake sitting on the table.

I didn't think much about it until my friend's little one bounced into the kitchen, grabbed the donut holes, and returned to Mom with a manipulative beg, "Mommy, can I have just one?" "Okay, just one," she replied. Five minutes later, "Mommy, can I have one?" he asked again with a steadfast dance. "Oh, just one more," she sighed, looking at me for acceptance.

This continued until he had eaten seven donut holes in the course of thirty minutes. I knew this wasn't going to be pretty, and it wasn't. His dance suddenly included jumping and jerking steps. The boy turned whiny and mean. He started crashing his cars into Bella until finally a full-fledged demolition derby broke out. Bella got scared. I got scared!

"He gets like this sometimes," his mother explained, attempting to settle him down.

I knew how and why he had turned from a manageable busy bee into a crazed hornet. Didn't she?

Excess sugar directly affects a body's chemistry and physiology, which in turn affect behavior, sleep, concentration, and several other bodily functions. How long the effects last, how intense they are, and even whether the body reacts much at all depend on an individual's makeup. I discovered this for myself in Eating Disorder Recovery 101. Months of strict food logging was also of great value to observing how my system reacted to certain foods—as well as Bella's.

This I know: Locking into what you know is best for a child's system and being keenly aware of the effects certain foods can have on it is essential. Let me share another example.

Our family doesn't eat out much, but we especially don't go out for or order in pizza. Pizza is a trigger food for my eating disorder. It is also full of salt, which causes Bella to swell up. Her tiny fingers and toes transform into chunky bratwursts, making her extremely cranky.

If we crave pizza, we make a homemade version. I offer a trouble-free pizza recipe later in this chapter.

Will Rogers once said, "Most of the time, things go better when you've got a plan." For our family, eating definitely goes better with a plan—a simple and balanced plan. I'll refer to and discuss our plan of eating simple staple foods. The foods cater nicely to Bella's sugar- and salt-sensitive system, as well as to my recovery. It also meets our family's sweet-tooth demands without making us feel deprived. Granted, my husband and other two children do not have extra busy, sugar-sensitive bodies, nor are they in recovery for an eating disorder. But experience has demonstrated that we are happier as a family, and Bella is more successful in adhering to the balanced diet, if everyone's on board. This rhythm of intentional eating works for us.

Simple Staple Foods

The upcoming pages list and discuss my family's simple staple foods. The foods are healthy and versatile in meal planning, and the recipes are relatively inexpensive. Keep in mind that appearance can make or break a meal, especially with extra busy *picky* eaters.

On a side note: I try very hard not ever to tell my children they can't have a certain food item that is off the plan. That makes them crave it even more. I teach moderation. Nonetheless, food recovery has taught me that if there is a certain food you know turns you or a child into a moody maniac or crazed hornet, don't risk keeping it in the house. The child will be less likely to want it if it isn't available.

Eating staple food may not appear appealing. Nevertheless, considering diet and exercise can help you understand extra busy behavior. If you think a correlation exists between an extra busy child's diet and his behavior, consult a physician before making any drastic changes in food and exercise. Diet management for children should always fall under the supervision of a doctor who can monitor the child's health and conduct periodic blood tests if needed (Umansky and Smalley 2003).

Staple Foods

Keep in mind food allergies when considering all staple foods.

Bananas: We eat literally bunches of bananas, mostly plain for breakfast and as an on-the-go-snack. My children scarf them down before athletic practices and in homemade smoothies. I mush up ripe ones in pancake batter and in tortillas with peanut butter. In the summertime my husband puts them on the grill to bake for dessert after barbecuing. I slice them into yogurt and over cereal as well. We enjoy bananas as a frozen treat too.

Beans: Beans are our fall and winter dinnertime staple food. I toss all sorts in the crock pot and let them go: pinto beans, navy beans, kidney beans, lentils, and split peas. I serve cornbread or biscuits alongside the dish. Bisquick brand biscuit mix offers great recipes for breads served as side dishes.

Beef: My children enjoy beef in pasta and brown rice as well as between two whole wheat sesame buns. It's a top source of protein, iron, and zinc. I disguise shredded carrots, onions, bell peppers, and even oatmeal in hamburgers. Blanketed with low-fat cheese, inside surprises are easily hidden. To eliminate a majority of fat from beef, I boil it. I seldom fry beef. After boiling, I add seasonings for additional flavor.

Brown Rice: Besides bananas, we consume a considerable amount of brown rice, especially in the spring and summer months. Did you know that brown rice has three times as much fiber as white rice? It's nutritious and inexpensive for our family of five. We enjoy brown rice with

- vegetables and chicken,
- beef and low-sodium soy sauce,
- a little butter,
- milk and cinnamon,
- scrambled eggs, and
- just plain.

Cantaloupe: This flexible melon can be served at any time of the day. Cubed, chilled, or served with a little whipped cream and sprinkles, cantaloupe can put a smile on any tiny face. Cantaloupe is a great calorie-wise food for extra busy children who need to lose a few pounds. Watermelon and honeydew are melons we enjoy regularly too. Use a melon scoop to form spheres for fruit kabobs, add chunks of bananas and other favorite fruits.

Carrots: Whether raw, stemmed, or served baby sized, carrots are full of beta carotene—vitamin A. Carrots are great as after school snacks, shredded in morning pancakes, or cooked with cinnamon.

Cereal: Children love cereal. The options available add up to aisles upon aisles. I suggest sticking to basics like Chex (all kinds), Cheerios, Kix, Corn Flakes, Grape Nuts, and Shredded Wheat. For a fun and lasting snack, mix cereals with raisins and other finger foods. Remember to check cereal labels. The ingredients are listed in order of quantity.

Chicken Breasts: We enjoy chicken breasts baked, grilled, marinated, and barbecued. I cube chicken for tortillas and serve it over rice with vegetables. Next to beef, we get a significant amount of our protein from chicken breasts. I list several fast chicken meals in the recipe section.

Diluted Orange Juice: Fresh, 100 percent squeezed OJ is one of the most nutritious juices possible, starring vitamin C, folate, and potassium. The calcium-fortified types are great for extra busy children who refuse milk. Be careful of orange juice wannabes—a.k.a, junk juice. Dilute it when possible. I dilute OJ because my children find it tart. Bella's enjoys 1/3 cup water mixed with 2/3 cup OJ. Add seltzer to orange juice for a quenching treat.

Eggs: My children enjoy eggs for breakfast on the weekends. Loaded with protein, eggs are fabulous as a snack too. They can be served many ways: scrambled with skim milk for a fluffy look, hard boiled for salads, or fried sunny-side up with cooking spray. Eggs also add flavor to brown rice. Just scramble and toss in.

Low-Fat Cheese: Low-fat cheese varieties include Swiss, Monterey Jack, white, and cheddar. String cheese comes in an assortment of low-fat flavors as well. One serving has lots of bone-building calcium. As a melted topping, cheese can make veggies or pasta more appealing to extra busy eaters. My children love Parmesan cheese lightly sprinkled on pasta, veggies, salads, eggs, and warm bread. In the recipe pages you'll discover a cheddar cheese sauce I drape over pasta.

Milk: Like most families with small children and teenagers (with bottomless stomachs), we consume a lot of milk. It seems as though every time I turn around I'm heading back to the grocery store for another gallon. We enjoy milk with cereal and oatmeal, and we drink it at most meals. We even paint with it on toast. Look for the tortilla- and toast-art recipes later in this chapter.

Oatmeal: This highly soluble, fiber-rich breakfast food is a big part of our morning diet. Bella loves her oatmeal runny—soupy looking. I prefer my oatmeal lumpy. My two older children enjoy cinnamon mixed in their oatmeal bowls. My husband will eat whatever oatmeal I put in front of him. I rely on quick-cooking oats, ready in five minutes. Rolled oats take a little longer. I seldom get picky about oatmeal. Oatmeal is oatmeal—good for the whole family. Farina (Cream of Wheat, for example) is another variety of hot cereal I serve with yogurt, toast, or fruit. The key to keeping oatmeal nutritious is not drowning it in sugar or butter.

Pancakes: Pancakes are a lifesaver. They are hearty, keeping children energized with fuel well into early afternoon. Pancakes can be prepared in all shapes (use cookie cutters) and sizes, or in a waffle iron. Plump blueberries, ripe bananas, or Grape Nuts cereal can turn pancakes into an even more delicious, warm, and pleasing meal by simply tossing the extra ingredients into the batter. The Bisquick box has a simple and quick "heart-smart" recipe I rely on. You can find it online.

Peanut Butter: This spread is very adaptable. We put it on and between bread, toast, tortillas, pancakes, and waffles. My children all love a good old-fashioned PB&J with a big glass of milk. I also thin out this protein-rich spread with water for my children to use as a dip for celery, cheese sticks, and bananas.

Popcorn and Pretzels: Our family consumes a lot of air-popped popcorn in place of potato chips. Bella enjoys dipping pretzels in yogurt or thinned out peanut butter. **Note**: Storing popcorn in a pantry is a no-no. Refrigerated popcorn pops better. Keep it cold.

Sweet Potatoes: Vitamin A roars in these taters. Slice sweet potatoes into strips, spray them lightly with cooking spray, and bake them—they become healthy fries. We enjoy sweet potatoes very lightly sprinkled with powdered sugar. You can also boil sweet potatoes, mash them and add milk, a dab of butter, and cinnamon. The creamier, the better. Pumpkin pie spice is divine sprinkled over a hot sweet potato.

Tuna (Canned) in Spring Water: Tuna is inexpensive, easy to prepare, and full of important nutrients extra busy children require. Add in that it's low in fat and calories when compared with other foods, and tuna is very close to being the perfect protein-rich food. My children enjoy tuna on whole wheat saltine crackers, whole wheat bread with low-fat cheese and fat-free mayonnaise, and in quick casseroles and cheese balls.

Whole Grain or Whole Wheat Pasta: I'm not a gifted cook. After vowing "I do," I could scarcely produce ice cubes. Preparing pasta was one of my first lessons in the kitchen. I played with all types: fettuccini, linguini, jumbo shells, macaroni, angel hair, rotini, and penne. To this day my children enjoy testing whether a pot of spaghetti noodles is done: They throw a wet noodle at the refrigerator. If it sticks, it's done. The possibilities for pasta dishes are vast, as are desired dressings. I seldom use store-bought sauces. As mentioned earlier, in the recipe section, you'll discover a basic cheese sauce—our noodle zest. I play with it, adding chicken, beef, vegetables, and different cheeses depending on the day, or whatever I have on hand. My children also respond well to plain pasta with minced and sautéed garlic served with warm, lightly buttered French bread.

Whole Wheat Bread: I started my children off with whole wheat bread at the very beginning because it's loaded with iron, zinc, and fiber. Extra busy children who have always eaten white bread may need to be weaned from it. Introduce whole wheat items incognito, using cheese or peanut butter. Use cookie cutters to make fun finger sandwiches to entice little eaters. I turn whole wheat bread into French toast or cinnamon toast at breakfast, and then use it for tuna cheese sandwiches at lunch. You'll never know if a child enjoys the taste of whole wheat bread unless you offer it.

Whole Wheat Tortillas: Versatile, low in fat, and long lasting in fuel, one can roll almost anything in these flattened whole wheat flour wonders. Bella enjoys tortillas wrapped around mayonnaise, cheese, and lettuce, then sliced into wheels. Tortillas are little-people friendly. They're great for extra busy bees who insist, "I can do it by myself!" Tortillas can also be whipped into quick quesadillas with beans and low-fat cheese, a favorite of my two older children. Use whole wheat pitas or corn tortillas for variety. Check labels; whole wheat flour should be listed first.

Yogurt: Yogurt is packed with calcium, but beware of brands swelling with sugar. Once again, check labels. Yogurt can be served many ways: parfaits with low-fat granola, topped with fruit, or mixed with Grape Nuts and berries. We enjoy yogurt served for breakfast with some whole wheat bread with peanut butter. Children also enjoy sprinkles on yogurt as a quick treat.

Sample Staple Recipes

Staple foods, regular water play, and lots of water consumption keep my family healthy and active. Use a variety of food textures in meals at home or at snacktime in the classroom for extra busy children to experience and enjoy. Excellent examples include salsa with extra cilantro, ice chips, chunked kiwi, sliced peaches, strawberries, raspberries, dill pickles, mustard, figs, crisp lettuce, rice cakes, Jell-O, applesauce, and lemon, lime, or orange wedges. Wooden craft sticks make fantastic serving sticks for sliced snacks. Just poke in and serve. The following staple food recipes are several of our favorites, and they contribute to our overall health.

Quick Chicken and Rice Soup

> 1 cup uncooked brown rice
> 1 cup mixed vegetables
> 6 cups chicken broth
> 2 teaspoons salt

Cook brown rice in chicken broth until rice is tender. Season to taste. Makes 8 servings. Add leftover chicken or boiled beef if desired. Sprinkle with grated low-fat cheese.

Quick Chicken Noodle Soup

> 16 oz. noodles
> 1 cup mixed vegetables
> 6 cups chicken broth

Cook noodles in chicken broth until noodles are tender. Add mixed vegetables. Season to taste. Makes 8 servings. Serve with baked chicken breasts and a salad.

Quick Noodle Meal #1

> 16 oz. noodles
> 2 cups pinto or kidney beans
> 1 cup mixed vegetables (optional)
> 1 ½ cups shredded low-fat cheese

Cook beans ahead of time. Keep warm. Cook noodles and drain. Keep warm. Add beans. Add mixed vegetables, if desired. Sprinkle cheese on top. (My children enjoy lots of cheese.) Serve with a salad and warm bread or biscuits.

Quick Noodle Meal #2

    16 oz. noodles
    ½ cup butter
    2 cups grated Parmesan cheese
    ½ teaspoon pepper

Cook and drain noodles. Add butter, Parmesan cheese, and pepper. Toss until cheese melts. Meal options: add cubed chicken breasts, a can of tuna, or a cup or two of boiled beef. Serve with a vegetable.

Mac 'n' Cheese Meal

    1 pound ground beef
    5 cups cooked noodles
    1 cup mixed vegetables (optional)
    1 cup shredded low-fat cheese

Cook noodles and drain. Boil ground beef until brown. Drain and rinse. Put in baking dish with noodles. Add mixed vegetables, if desired. Cover with cheese and desired pasta sauce. The cheddar cheese sauce recipe below is delicious. Bake at 325 degrees for 40 minutes.

Cheddar Cheese Sauce

    ¼ cup grated cheddar cheese (other low-fat cheese options
       work too)
    2 tablespoons flour
    ¼ teaspoon salt
    ½ cup skim milk
    1 cup chicken broth

Boil ½ cup chicken broth in saucepan. After adding a small amount of cold broth to the flour, add to saucepan and cook until it bubbles. Add milk and remaining chicken broth gradually and stir until thickened. Add the grated cheese. Season with salt and pepper. This sauce is great over any pasta.

Sweet Tater Soup

6 cups diced, uncooked sweet potatoes

1 cup diced celery

1 cup diced carrots

1 cup peas

1 cup diced onion

4 cups skim milk

In sauce pan combine all of the veggies. Cover with water and cook until tender. Drain. Add milk and heat until hot. Season with salt and pepper. Add cubed chicken if desired. Serve with a salad and bread.

Sweet Tater Cakes

4 large sweet potatoes, grated coarsely

½ onion, finely grated

2 eggs

¼ cup flour

1 teaspoon salt

Add eggs and onions to grated potatoes. Stir until blended. Add flour and salt. Use large spoon to measure batter and fry in skillet with desired amount and variety of oil until brown on both sides. Serve plain or with a little butter. My children also enjoy sweet tater cakes as a reheated snack.

Tuna Cheese Balls

1 8 oz. can tuna in spring water

3 cups whole wheat Bisquick mix

4 cups shredded low-fat cheese (any variety)

½ cup Parmesan cheese

Mix all ingredients together. Shape into 1-inch balls. Place on a lightly greased pan. Bake in a 325 degree oven for 25 to 30 minutes. Serve warm. Dip in cheddar cheese sauce (recipe above) if desired.

The following recipes do not require precise measurements. Use the kind of toppings or vegetables the children like.

Baked Bananas

One banana per person works best. Place whole, unpeeled banana on a baking sheet in a 325-degree oven. Bake for 35 minutes. Peel bananas. Serve with honey, cinnamon, or pumpkin pie spice.

Baked Oriental Chicken

Cut chicken into bite-size pieces and soak in low-sodium soy sauce for several hours. Sauté in olive oil with onions, bell peppers, and shredded carrots. Transfer to a baking pan and bake, covered, at 325 degrees for about 45 minutes. Serve with a side salad and brown rice.

Homemade Pizza

Busy Bag Trick
Use saltine crackers in place of English muffins for bite-size pizzas. Children love the mini treats.

For crusts, use whole wheat English muffin halves or a whole wheat tortilla cut into quarters. Spread a little leftover cheddar cheese sauce on each. Top with an assortment of chopped veggies and cheeses. Microwave until cheese melts. Add a veggie smiley face for added excitement.

Sleep Matters

To function and develop properly, extra busy children require healthy sleeping habits. Several restless nights have demonstrated that Bella is more attentive, less grouchy, and overall a more pleasant child when she is well rested. Lack of sleep causes her three core busy habits—excessive movement, noise, and stubbornness—to escalate significantly. A child who is sleep deprived may exhibit the following:

- Loses focus—wanders from one activity to another
- Seeks stimulation to keep going—annoys siblings or pets, wants to watch TV, especially in the late afternoon
- Needs your attention and help to stay on task
- Is forgetful
- Struggles to make decisions
- Doesn't listen
- Has difficulty performing at peak levels or resists participating altogether
- Talks excessively
- Finds it difficult to work without disrupting others

(Kurcinka 2006, 24)

In her book, *The 7 O'clock Bedtime* (2001), Inda Schaenen presents compelling evidence regarding the correlation between problematic behavior and sleep deprivation. She draws from many sources, all worth adding to your Busy Bag.

In *Solve Your Child's Sleep Problems* (1985), Richard Ferber writes, "In fact all of us, regardless of age, function best when we keep regular schedules. Studies in adults have shown that irregular sleep-wake patterns lead to significant alterations in our moods and sense of well-being, and undermine our ability to sleep at desired times. The same is true of young children" (44).

In his book, *Healthy Sleep Habits, Happy Child* (1999), Marc Weissbluth writes, "Sleep deficiency in childhood may harm neurological development, and the problems might not show up until later. I think it is possible that unhealthy sleep habits contribute to school-related problems such as attention deficit hyperactivity disorder (ADHD) and learning disabilities. I also suspect that chronically tired children become chronically tired adults who suffer in ways we can't measure: less resiliency, less ability to cope with life's stresses, less curiosity, less empathy, less playfulness. The message here is simple: Sleep is a powerful modifier of behavior, performance, and personality" (xix).

According to the Sleep Medicine and Research Center in St. Louis, children—extra busy or not—require the following sleeping hours for each day:

- One-year-old: fourteen hours, including one or two naps
- Two-year-old: eleven to twelve hours at night plus a single, after-lunch nap of one to two hours
- Three-year-old: twelve to twelve and a half hours
- Four-year-old: eleven and a half to twelve hours
- Five-year-old: eleven hours
- Six-year-old: ten and three-quarters to eleven hours
- Seven-year-old: ten and a half to eleven hours
- Eight-year-old: ten and a quarter to ten and three quarters hours

(Schaenen 2001, 150)

Ideas for Helping Extra Busy Children Sleep Better

As a parent of an extra busy child, I believe poor nighttime sleep causes poor daytime behavior. You may or may not agree. I'm up for sharing Bella after a restless night or two for persuasion purposes.

Below are several suggestions to share with families for helping extra busy children maintain healthy sleeping habits:

- **Establish a regular bedtime routine.**

  It should prompt the child through each step of getting ready for bed. Develop a visually cued routine and stick consistently to it, even on the weekends. Playing sleep catch up can be hard on an extra busy child's system. I've been there and done that! Start as early as needed. Bella can draw bedtime out with every excuse imaginable, including a sudden tummy ache and these imaginative quotes:

  > "My water had floaties in it. I need another drink."
  >
  > "Bless Mommy, Daddy, PJ, Farrah, Mr. Sartin, Miss Franny, Julie, Victoria, and . . ." everyone else in her six-year-old extra busy world.

  I discuss a transitioning bedtime game and dig deeper into bedtime routines a few pages ahead.

- **Cut off eating at an appropriate time.**

  Most parents know what will or will not send their child into a sugar frenzy. I strongly recommend not giving an extra busy child a soda or anything similar thirty minutes prior to starting a bedtime routine. Heavy snacking right before bed isn't recommended. If a child is hungry, offer graham crackers and yogurt.

- **Monitor what a child views on TV before bed.**

  Bella caught the end of a Goosebumps episode PJ was watching one afternoon. Although R. L. Stein's series isn't Stephen King, it spooked Bella for several nights. I suggest avoiding spooky stories too. Children can and do experience night terrors and nightmares, disrupting healthy sleep patterns. For more information on both topics check into Mary Sheedy Kurcinka's *Sleepless in America: Is Your Child Misbehaving or Missing Sleep?* (2006).

- **Allow the child a night-light if needed.**

  Being afraid of the dark is common for children. Night-lights help children feel secure, and many often sleep better with one.

- **Keep the house quiet**.

  This is common sense. A blasting TV or stereo will not allow a child to sleep.

- **Have the child wear pajamas**.

  Also, make sure the room isn't too hot or too cold. Sleeping time is often no exception to busyness. Kinesthetic children can squirm and kick off their blankets while sleeping. Children who are chilly or too warm are naturally cheated out of valuable z's.

- **Turn the phone ringer off**.

  Do this especially if evening calls are a problem. Have a teenager? Enforce a phone curfew to remedy the problem.

- **Don't wrestle before bed**.

  My husband is guilty of this on several counts. He often affectionately "loves" on Bella while tucking her in at night with a game called "Who's My Everlasting Gobstopper?" This game involves rubbing noses together and Daddy raspberry kissing Bella's cheeks. Of course the game riles her up, and that deviates from the needed calmness for bedtime. Once again, steer clear of high-energy activities before bed.

- **Don't get wishy-washy about bedtime routines**.

  Many parents, after being away from their children all day, give in to requests for just one more story or just twenty more minutes. This undermines needed consistency and authority. Be gentle. Be firm. Be consistent.

- **Lock into a child's sleeping cues**.

  A yawn or heavy bobbing head may indicate an earlier bedtime is needed—at least during transitioning periods such as changes to and from daylight savings time or visiting relatives during the holidays.

- **Be careful of doling out over-the-counter cold medication at bedtime**.

  Many are coated with alcohol, and even nonalcohol versions can initiate strong reactions from little bodies needing sleep. Try vitamin C tablets; they have numerous benefits.

Busy Bag Trick

An additional sleep resource to add to your Busy Bag is *Sleep: The Brazelton Way* by T. Berry Brazelton and Joshua D. Sparrow (2003). It's loaded with even more practical tips and advice on children's individual sleeping needs and patterns.

- **Keep extra busy children out of your bed.**
  You probably won't get a good night's sleep, which is vital for keeping up with extra busy children. Besides, children benefit from being in their own bed for consistency purposes.

And remember
- Extra busy children are more careless and accident prone when not well rested.
- Extra busy children are susceptible to lingering viruses when not well rested.
- Extra busy children who don't sleep well don't grow and develop well.
- Extra busy children function better in the classroom when properly rested.
- Extra busy children who sleep well usually have parents and teachers who sleep well.

Bedtime Routines

I wish I could say I've been completely successful with my children's sleeping patterns and habits. I was inconsistent and wishy-washy with PJ and Farrah. But Bella, well, we've had better luck with her because of our two prior attempts. This we've learned from them: to effectively meet a child's sleep requirements, a consistent bedtime routine is important for winding down each day. Let's look closely at Bella's bedtime routine for connection point purposes.

At 8:00 PM I inform Bella she is to start getting ready for bed. Actually, my exact words are, "Bella, it's time to pick out a bedtime story." I usually have to get up and physically help her transition to her room to select a book from her big book box. (Books in her big bedroom book box are purposely selected short stories, lasting about five minutes. She has a shelf downstairs I rotate her books through.)

After she selects her bedtime book, it's about 8:10 and time to put on her pajamas. I keep this simple by having her choices ready. "Bella, you can wear your red pj's or your blue pj's." I keep her choices to two. It's 8:15 by now, and she's off to brush her teeth. This takes about five minutes. By 8:20, Bella is in her bed, ready for a story. Interaction with the book puts us at 8:30 for beginning kisses, hugs, and a question or two about her day. She has a drink of water at about 8:35. Then the night-light is switched on. An extra kiss is given. The lights are turned out. Double-tucks come at around 8:45. (Bella likes to have her daddy or me come back in her room and tell her what the next morning holds—a school day, church day, or sleeping-in day.) Bella is asleep before 9:00 most nights. She is wakened at 7:00 AM for school, which allows her little body adequate sleep for repair, growth, and recovery from the prior day.

Before I go any further, I'd like to emphasize that you try not to get caught up in the time, the exact minutes, during the unfolding of a bedtime routine. Some nights you may need to allow more time to get through the routine than others. I have found that the value of a bedtime routine is in the consistency of each step, not whether it is done in exactly twenty, twenty-five, or thirty minutes. Bella's bedtime routine is started early enough to accommodate a slow or uncooperative start. You'll soon see that firmness doesn't mean being unbendable to daily demands. Listed below are suggestions for creating a calm and orderly bedtime routine, one that has meaning and closes an extra busy child's day on a positive note:

- **Start bedtime off with a bath.**

  Many of my friends begin their children's bedtime routines with warm baths. I don't bathe Bella daily. Some may scoff, but I bathe her on Sunday and Wednesday nights during the winter. I add Fridays during warmer weather months. When Bella does receive a bath—a "tubby"—she really looks forward to when she does. Her bathing rituals will change when puberty sets in. Nonetheless, a tubby is a soothing and relaxing way to begin a bedtime routine.

- **Make story time a part of bedtime**.

  As an educator I highly recommend reading to children, or telling stories, as a component of bedtime. Not only are the benefits of both innumerable, the possibilities are as well. Read classics such as *Goodnight Moon* by Margaret Wise Brown, chapter books like *Charlotte's Web* by E. B. White (read a chapter a night), poetry, folk tales, or even make-believe stories created together. Children will naturally be lured through a bedtime routine if anticipating a final book chapter or the ending to a captivating story.

- **Turn off the TV**.

  If the TV is on when bedtime rolls around, turn it off. It can only act as a distraction. Sleep experts recommend turning the television off an hour before bedtime to set the stage for settling down. Play soft music instead, or dim the lights, to put the child in a relaxing mood for his bedtime ritual.

- **Give bedtime routines a theme or kick every once in a while**.

  During the summer, I let Bella sleep in one of her daddy's T-shirts. His scent and the shirt's natural body-wrapping feel put her gently to sleep. On Valentine's Day, put hearts on the ceiling. On a child's birthday, let her select two bedtime stories or sing her a birthday lullaby.

- **Omit the phrase "time for bed."**

  Some children naturally get turned off when they hear someone say, "Time for bed." Try a different approach. "Last one upstairs in their pajamas is a rotten egg!" Or coax the child with the continuation of a story. "Fredricka, tonight we get to finish our special bedtime story, 'The Adventures of Milton and Maggie.'" A close friend of mine starts her extra busy boy's bedtime ritual off with "Ready or not here I come!" This cues the child to stop what he is doing, clean up (of course), and go find a hiding spot in a designated room. His mom seeks him out with his pajamas in hand.

- **Play simple games**.

  Playing a simple game before tucking a child in can initiate an incentive to get ready for bed. Here's an effortless one:

cup   cake   cupcake

compound word puzzles. To play, think of compound words and draw them in addition problem form similar to Bella's example above. Keep a small pad and pencil on the child's nightstand or a nearby drawer for simple games of Tic-Tac-Toe or Hangman.

Or play Race the Clock during particular periods of a bedtime routine. "Elton, let's see how fast you can put on your pajama bottoms." Children get into the game if a stopwatch is used. I don't recommend Race the Clock for toothbrushing.

- **Employ magical mist.**

 "But I can't sleep!" I'm sure this phrase is commonly heard by the parents of extra busy children. Rather than replying, "Camille, just go to sleep," redirect the comment by asking the child if she needs a magical misting of sleeping juice. To magically mist, fill a misting plant water bottle and gently spray the child from above. Sing a soft lullaby. "Hush Little Baby" is a common favorite.

- **Gently massage the child.**

 Some children are more eager to follow a bedtime routine if a foot and toe ("piggy") massage is involved. Use lavender lotion. While massaging, let the child rub some on a favorite stuffed animal for a lingering scent. Tell a story while massaging.

- **Use the ceiling fan**.

  As stated in chapter 1, ceiling fans can considerably soothe children. If available, turn on a child's ceiling fan right after kisses and story time to lull him to sleep.

- **Allow security items**.

  Bella sleeps with a soft lamb named "Laaaambert." She enjoys snuggling with it throughout the night. Most children enjoy and sleep better with security items. Allow one or two.

- **Don't rush a child's bedtime routine**.

  I try every night to make Bella's routine as calming and connecting as possible. Some nights I succeed. Others I do not. Nonetheless, our most successful nights are those left unhurried. If bedtime is rushed more times than not, start earlier.

- **Cue the end of a bedtime routine**.

  Whether a kiss, prayer, music box, book, or story, bedtime should have a consistent finale. Preferably one with an "I love you."

- **Use a bedtime routine check-off card**.

  Bedtime routines can run more smoothly with a check-off card for the child. One can be found in appendix B.

- **Don't carry over problems**.

  If bedtime doesn't run as smoothly as you would have liked on certain nights, don't carry the problem to the extra busy child's morning routine. Note the problem, and work at it one small step at a time.

In Closing . . .

Before venturing into chapter 7, remember that a child's sleeping and eating patterns greatly affect her play and learning patterns. As an educator you can help meet an extra busy child's nutrition and sleep requirements by making suggestions to parents as you deem appropriate. The Strengthening the Home-School Connection tidbits throughout this book are suitable to include in monthly newsletters home. And if all else fails, model, model, and model—even healthier eating during snack time. Post a food pyramid in your classroom. Go over it thoroughly with your students. Make it a point to teach them the benefits of healthy eating and adequate rest. They may not thank you now, but they will remember you for it when they are adults. For further nutrition and sleep suggestions for children, extra busy children included, check out the following resources:

Early Sprouts: Cultivating Healthy Food Choices in Young Children by Karrie Kalich, Dottie Bauer, and Deirdre McPartlin (2009)
What Are We Feeding Our Kids? by Michael F. Jacobson and Bruce Maxwell (1994)
American Academy of Pediatrics Guide to Your Child's Sleep: Birth through Adolescence edited by George J. Cohen (1999)

7

Let's Wrap Up

My undergraduate history courses introduced me to Samuel Plimsoll, an 1870s British leader who passed a law requiring all cargo ships to bear a visible mark above their waterline. If the waterline went above the mark, the ship was overloaded. Excess cargo had to be removed for the safety of those aboard. The mark became known as a Plimsoll mark. A major part of supporting a child's extra busy nature is keeping an eye on his Plimsoll mark. The analogy is simple. Like the ship, a kinesthetic child is more than likely overwhelmed if he is continually observed barely keeping his head above water—bobbing at the Plimsoll mark, so to speak. Several factors may be causing the child's Plimsoll mark to hit unmanageable status; mostly apparent is an obvious increase in busyness. At this point, initiating support for the extra busy child is necessary.

An Obvious Increase in Busyness

The following questions should be considered if an extra busy child begins drowning in extra busy habits:

- **Is there trouble or change at home or school?**

  Insert a stressful situation where consistency and harmony once flowed, and a child's behavior will change—nine times out of ten—especially if it is a situation with significant stress levels, such as a divorce or death in the family. A major move could also be extremely bothersome to a child. Other troublesome changes include getting a new teacher halfway through the year, the birth of a sibling, moving to a new school, getting a new caregiver or new neighbors, experiencing the death of a pet, having a parent always gone, or experiencing sibling rivalry.

- **Is a learning disability surfacing?**

  A learning disability can be defined as a disorder in the ability to process information, resulting in attention, perception, or memory deficits. Children with learning disabilities experience difficulty learning in school despite adequate hearing, vision, and intelligence (Lewis and Doorlag 1995). Children with learning disabilities, particularly in the primary grades, can display

  —distractibility

  —carelessness

  —poor organizational skills

  —poor coordination

  —poor fine and gross motor skills

  —poor reading and writing skills (usually first to surface)

  —poor self-esteem

  —frustration

  Work closely with the child's family and special-education teachers to evaluate her for a learning disability. If a disability is present, the sooner it is identified the better.

- **Are sensory problems a possibility?**

  Sensory problems could be to blame for an obvious increase in extra busy habits. Possible sensory problems might become apparent in the following ways:

  —A child is very sensitive to noise. A normal or relatively low volume hurts his ears or is intensely bothersome to him.

—A child is severely agitated by certain food textures and can identify the texture even in casseroles.

—A child has an extremely high or low tolerance for pain.

—A child strongly dislikes wearing certain textures of clothing, such as cotton or corduroy. Tags or ribbed seams can also be troublesome to extra busy children.

—A child is intensely afraid of water or heights.

I suggest that parents contact their child's pediatrician with questions. And I recommend two excellent books to check out on the topic.

Sensational Kids: Hope and Help for Children with Sensory Processing Disorder (SPD) by Lucy Jane Miller with Doris A. Fuller (2006)

The Everything Parent's Guide to Sensory Integration Disorder by Terri Mauro and Sharon A. Cermak (2006)

- **Is the child getting enough sleep?**
Without my necessary amount of z's, I become what my children call a "grumpy-pants." Few people function properly without adequate sleep, especially children. I discuss daily sleep recommendations for children in chapter 6.

- **Is the child's system sensitive or allergic to certain foods?**
Bella is sensitive to excess sugar and salt. We monitor her intake closely because of the obvious irritability and moodiness it stirs up in her. Are new flavors being tried that might not be sitting well with the child? Have you or the family switched brands on certain food items? Is Grandma visiting and doing the cooking?

- **How does your teaching style impact the child?**
Please don't underestimate your role in *making or breaking* a child's school year. How do you run your classroom? What kind of classroom environment is your child experiencing daily? Is it an overstimulated or understimulated classroom? Are there too many students in the classroom? Is the classroom poorly organized? Is the classroom environment competitive? Are rules vague and unclear? Has a substitute teacher been filling in?

Strengthening the Home-School Connection

An extra busy child may be having school troubles if the following is regularly occurring or heard at home:

"I have a stomachache. Can I stay home today?"

"I hate school!"

"I forgot my homework."

"I don't have any papers to show you."

- **Is the child's personality to blame?**

  Farrah, our middle child, was an extremely grumpy baby. She wasn't friendly as a toddler either. I worried this would be the case as she went off to grade school. Quite the opposite occurred. She grew out of her grouchy temperament. Could this be the case for the child you are thinking about?

- **Is the child just sick, tired, or hungry?**

  Hunger and fatigue can alter a child's behavior and performance in school. I mentioned earlier how combined hunger and exhaustion can bring out the worst in children. Children who aren't getting enough rest are more susceptible to colds and viruses, which run them down easily.

- **What does the child's daily diet look like?**

  Poor nutrition can change a child's mood. What exactly is the child consuming? How much water does the child drink, especially compared to soda? Is the child eating enough fruits and vegetables to keep her bowels regular? Suggest to parents that they log everything the child eats, as closely as possible, for two to three days. Look carefully at what they wrote down. Is it in the same ballpark as the nutritional recommendations for children?

- **Are low iron levels to blame?**

  Irritability can set in if iron levels decline, especially in children. Other symptoms of a low iron level include a lack of concentration, shortened attention span, and impaired cognitive skills. Low blood sugar can also cause irritability (Umansky and Smalley 2003, 36). The child's pediatrician should be contacted if there is concern about a low iron level.

- **Is the child's routine sliding?**

  When school is not in session it can be difficult for families to keep children on track with their schedules. As trying as it may be at times, consistency in routines is best for extra busy children. Slacking of any sort will usually result in an obvious increase in busyness. Before school breaks, encourage families to stick to their routines.

Busy Bag Trick

Reading age-appropriate books to extra busy children is an effective way to help them identify and understand awkward and uncomfortable feelings, especially during intense periods of busyness.

Anger *Alexander and the Terrible, Horrible, No Good, Very Bad Day* by Judith Viorst (1972)

Jealousy *One Frog Too Many* by Mercer Mayer and Marianna Mayer (1975)

Embarrassment *Loudmouth George and the Big Race* by Nancy Carlson (1983)

Fear *There's a Nightmare in My Closet* by Mercer Mayer (1968)

Sadness *The Tenth Good Thing about Barney* by Judith Viorst (1971)

- **Are there any additional possible causes**?

  Here is a list of additional possible causes to look for when there is an obvious increase in extra busy habits.

  —allergies

  —anger from within

  —anxiety

  —boredom

  —defiance

  —fears

  —frustration

  —jealousy

  —lack of discipline or not enough discipline

  —peer pressure

  —seasonal concerns

  —seeking attention

A Few Final Thoughts

At times, while I am tucking her into bed, Bella asks, "Mommy, why am I so little and PJ and Farrah are so big?" In her six-year-old, extra busy, precocious way, Bella has noticed the almost decade age difference between herself and her siblings. My answer is always the same: "Do you know you are the biggest surprise Mommy and Daddy ever received? Better than any Christmas or birthday present. We didn't know how much we needed you in our family until you came along. That is how special you are." Bella's unique nature and busyness have considerably grounded my husband and me in many areas. Teaching extra busy kinesthetic children cemented my thoughts even more. Several things are now crystal clear:

- Take each day as it comes.
- Children grow quickly.
- Children are very impressionable.
- Things happen for a reason.

- Patience is a virtue.
- Don't worry about what other people think.
- Think outside the box.
- Breathe deeply and regularly throughout the day.
- Do one thing daily to release stress.
- Squeeze humor and play in as much as possible.
- Share your passions with others, especially children.

The picture above of my husband and our three children was taken in 2003. As you may recall, it was a difficult year. Although a trying time, I focused on the good health and beauty of my family with one continual thought in mind: when all is said and done, tomorrow is another day.

And One More Thing . . .

If you're ever in my neck of the woods, Farmington, New Mexico, and you see a little red 2006 Ford Focus with a small dent on the right side zipping around, it's me. Bella will probably be in the back shuffling through her Keep 'Em Busy bag. Pull us over. We can swap stories and ideas about our similar extra busy experiences. You can peek in my Busy Bag, and I will definitely peek in yours.

Until then, I truly believe your efforts will be blessed, as will your attempts at a more creative and nurturing style of teaching and/or parenting. It's my hope that *Ants in Their Pants: Teaching Children Who Must Move to Learn* has been helpful, or that at least it made you smile, knowing we both can claim BTDT—been there, done that! We've lived, learned, and loved—and nurtured a lot of kinesthetic extra busy children too.

Appendix A

Helping Parents of Extra Busy Children

1. Always make it obvious that you want the best for the child. Let your actions support your words.

2. Share daily successes and setbacks, but keep in mind that parents do not want to be bombarded daily with everything their child is doing wrong. Use note cards, e-mail, a phone call, or a communication notebook for daily reports.

3. Always thank parents for spending time in your classroom or for returning phone calls. It will encourage continuing the behavior.

4. Send out regular invitations for parent involvement in the classroom and curriculum. A parent who is a police officer could visit as a guest speaker. Make a point of inviting parents with differing ethnic backgrounds for presentations.

5. Ask for feedback. What do they see as working best? Or not so well?

6. Be flexible and supportive.

7. Don't judge or criticize.

8. Get to know parents as people, not just as "Gloria's dad" or "Ricky's mom."

9. Keep in mind that parents and teachers are allies. As a team, teachers and parents can drastically improve the quality

Busy Bag Trick
To discuss and connect with classroom issues in a neutral way, host an afternoon coffee break for parents.

of an extra busy child's life and education. It is important to understand each other's perspectives though, making communication key.

Helping Teachers of Extra Busy Children

Parents of extra busy children can help teachers in many ways. For example

1. Go to all scheduled conferences.
2. Visit or volunteer in the classroom as much as possible.
3. Go on field trips.
4. Be a room parent to help with parties and learning centers.
5. Start a communication notebook.
6. Be flexible and supportive.
7. Offer suggestions, but realize that the educator ultimately manages the classroom.
8. Be open-minded, remembering that your child isn't the only child in the classroom.
9. Don't judge or criticize.
10. Remember that communication is key.

Appendix B

Calendar

Child's name: _____   Month: _____

Monday	Tuesday	Wednesday	Thursday	Friday

Comments: _____

Logging Page

Child's name: _____ Date: _____

Antecedent (before behavior)	
Behavior	
Consequence (after behavior)	

Comments: _____

_____

_____

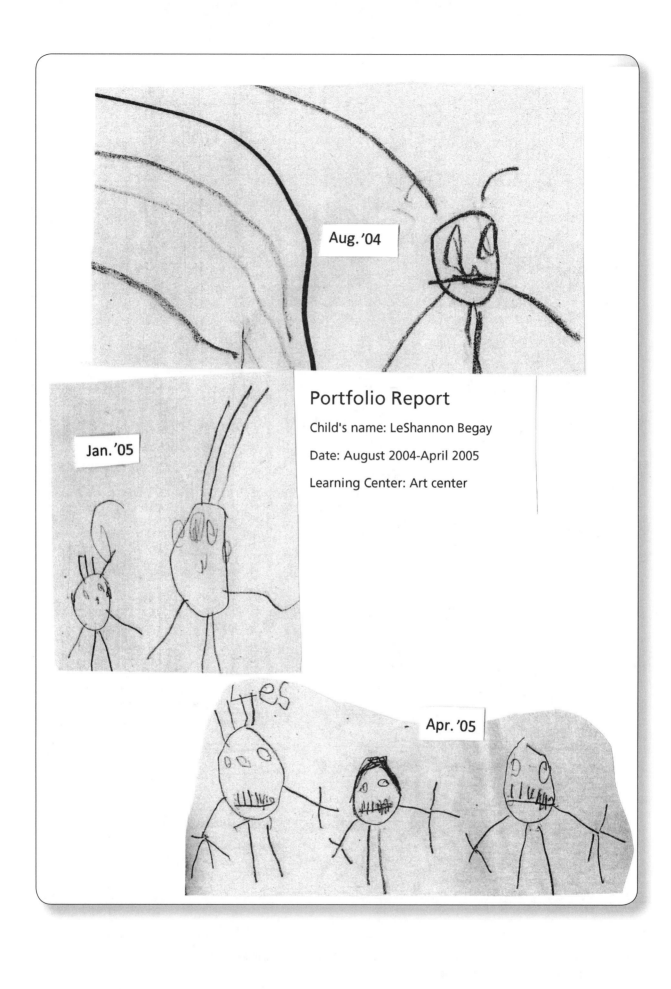

Aug. '04

Jan. '05

Apr. '05

Portfolio Report

Child's name: LeShannon Begay

Date: August 2004-April 2005

Learning Center: Art center

Portfolio Report

Child's name: LeShannon Begay

Date: May 2004-May 2005

Learning Center: Writing center

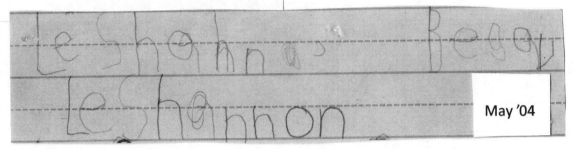

May '04

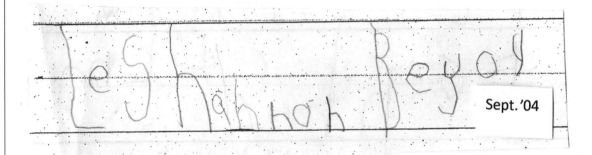

Sept. '04

Dec. '04

May '05

Bedtime Check-Off Card

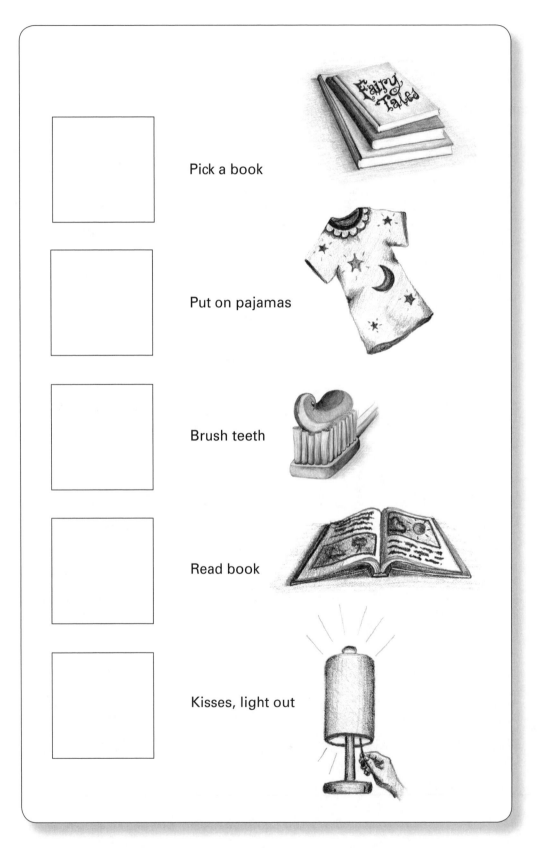

Pick a book

Put on pajamas

Brush teeth

Read book

Kisses, light out

References

Carlton, E. 2000. Learning through music: The support of brain research. *Exchange* 133 (May/June): 53–56.

Ferber, R. 1985. *Solve your child's sleep problems.* New York: Simon & Schuster.

Franzini, L. 2002. *Kids who laugh: How to develop your child's sense of humor.* Garden City Park, NY: Square One Publishers.

Good, L., J. Feekes, and B. Shawd. 1993. Let your fingers do the talking: Hands-on language learning through signing. *Childhood Education* 70 (2): 81–83.

Herrell, A., and M. Jordan 2004. *Fifty strategies for teaching English language learners.* 2nd ed. Upper Saddle River, NJ: Pearson/Merrill Prentice Hall.

Joseph, G. E., and P. S. Strain. 2003. Comprehensive evidence-based social-emotional curricula for young children: An analysis of efficacious adoption potential. *Topics in Early Childhood Special Education* 23 (2): 65–76.

Kennedy, P., L. Terdal, and L. Fusetti. 1993. *The hyperactive child book: A pediatrician, a child psychologist, and a mother team up to offer the most practical, up-to-date guide to treating, educating, and living with your ADHD child.* New York: St. Martin's Press.

Kostelnik, M. 1993. Recognizing the essentials of developmentally appropriate practice. *Child Care Information Exchange* 90 (3): 73–77.

Kranowitz, C. S. 1992. Catching preschoolers before they fall: A developmental screening. *Child Care Information Exchange* 84:25–26.

———. 1995. *101 activities for kids in tight spaces: At the doctor's office, on car, train, and plane trips, home sick in bed . . .* New York: St. Martin's Press.

Kurcinka, M. S. 2006. *Sleepless in America: Is your child misbehaving or missing sleep?* New York: HarperCollins.

Lewis R., and D. Doorlag. 1995. *Teaching special students in the mainstream.* Englewood Cliffs, NJ: Merrill.

Louv, R. 2005. *Last child in the woods: Saving our children from nature-deficit disorder.* Updated and expanded edition. Chapel Hill, NC: Algonquin Books.

Mauro, T., and S. A. Cermak. 2006. *The everything parent's guide to sensory integration disorder: Get the right diagnosis, understand treatments, and advocate for your child.* Avon, MA: Adams Media.

Maxine, D. 1998. Aquatic therapy for children [electronic version]. Abilitations and the Aquatic Therapy and Rehab Institute. http://www.transitioncoalition.org/transition/ moca/2006resourcedirectgcd.oa.mo.gov/pdf2006resourcedirectory .pdf.

Rosenow, N. 2005. The impact of sensory integration on behavior: Discovering our best selves. *Child Care Information Exchange* 164:55–8.

Schaenen, I. 2001. *The 7 o'clock bedtime.* New York: Regan Books.

Shapiro, L. E. 2003. *The secret language of children: How to understand what your kids are really saying.* Naperville, IL: Sourcebooks, Inc.

Stoppard, M. 2001. *Teach your child: How to discover and enhance your child's true potential.* New York: DK Publishing, Inc.

Trent, J. T., J. DuFour Love, and C. Trent. 1998. *The treasure tree.* Nashville, TN: Tommy Nelson.

Umansky, W., and B. Smalley. 2003. *AD/HD: Helping your child.* New York: Warner Books.

Weissbluth, M. 1999. *Healthy sleep habits, happy child: A step-by-step program for a good night's sleep*. Second revised edition. New York: Ballantine Books.

Whelchel, L. 2000. *Creative correction: Extraordinary ideas for everyday discipline*. Wheaton, IL: Tyndale House.

Wilcox, S., and P. Wilcox. 1997. *Learning to see: Teaching American Sign Language as a second language*. 2nd ed. Washington, DC: Gallaudet University Press.

Wong, H. K., and R. T. Wong. 2001. *The first days of school: How to be an effective teacher*. Mountain View, CA: Harry K. Wong Publications.